Peter Hardelle
with love from Susan
November 1987.

CHANGE & DECAY
The Future of Our Churches

CHANGE & DECAY
The Future of Our Churches

Marcus Binney
and Peter Burman

Studio Vista
London

PHOTO CREDITS

A Studio Vista book published by
Cassell & Collier Macmillan Publishers Ltd,
35 Red Lion Square, London WC1R 4SG
and at Sydney, Auckland, Toronto, Johannesburg,
an affiliate of
Macmillan Publishing Co. Inc.,
New York

ISBN 0 289 70774 9 (Hardback)
ISBN 0 289 70775 7 (Paperback)
Designed by Brooke Snell
Set in Monophoto Ehrhardt 9pt
Filmset and printed in Great Britain by
BAS Printers Limited, Wallop, Hampshire
Bound by Webb & Sons Ltd

CONTENTS

GLOSSARY

Official Bodies

GENERAL SYNOD of the Church of England is the 'parliament' of the Church, which is responsible for the government of the Anglican Church in the forty-three English dioceses. It enacts legislation in the form of Measures, which, having been debated and passed by the Synod, are then submitted to both Houses of Parliament, and when passed by Parliament, receive the Royal Assent and become part of English statute law.

CHURCH COMMISSIONERS for England are the trustee body for the ancient central endowments of the Church of England; the senior Commissioners are three Church Estates Commissioners, the second being an appointee of the government of the day, and answerable for the Commissioners in Parliament.

COUNCIL FOR PLACES OF WORSHIP (formerly Council for the Care of Churches) of the General Synod is the coordinating body of the Diocesan Advisory Committees for the care of churches. The Council advises on the architectural and historic merits of churches being considered for redundancy under the Pastoral Measure, and counsels chancellors and DACs on matters of difficulty.

DIOCESAN ADVISORY COMMITTEES (DACs) were established shortly after the First World War to advise diocesan chancellors on the architectural, archaeological, artistic and historical aspects of applications for faculties.

PASTORAL COMMITTEES advise the bishop in each diocese on the pastoral supervision needed 'to make better provision for the care of souls', and are called on to consider the best and wisest deployment of the Church's resources of manpower, buildings and money, in order that adequate services and pastoral care can be maintained.

DIOCESAN REDUNDANT CHURCHES USES COMMITTEES (commonly referred to as 'uses committees') were established by the Pastoral Measure, 1968, to seek suitable proposals for alternative uses for those churches which are legally declared redundant. They often include architects, surveyors and estate agents among their members, and report offers of alternative uses to the Church Commissioners, on whom the final decisions rest.

ADVISORY BOARD FOR REDUNDANT CHURCHES advises the Church Commissioners on the architectural and historic quality of all redundant and potentially redundant Anglican churches. It may grant Demolition Certificates (*q.v.*) and also advises the Commissioners on the architectural propriety of schemes for the conversion of redundant churches for alternative use.

REDUNDANT CHURCHES FUND preserves 'in the interests of the Nation and the Church of England' those churches of historic and architectural merit which the Church Commissioners, on the advice of the Advisory Board, decide to vest in it.

REPRESENTATIVE BODY of the Church in Wales was created following the disestablishment of the Church in Wales to hold property on behalf of the church and fulfils a role analagous to that of the Church Commissioners in relation to redundant churches.

Grants and Grant-Giving Bodies

PILGRIM TRUST, HAYWARD FOUNDATION AND THE RADCLIFFE TRUST are outstanding among the private charitable foundations which give grants for the conservation of artistic treasures in churches or towards the maintenance of specialist techniques.

HISTORIC CHURCHES PRESERVATION TRUST was established in 1953 as a national grant-giving body able to help historic churches of merit of all denominations; since its establishment it has dispensed some £2½m in grant aid. In addition to the HCPT some 18 counties have affiliated County Trusts which, albeit mostly on a modest scale, support the efforts of the parent body by locally directed effort.

FRIENDS OF FRIENDLESS CHURCHES is a smaller but effective body which channels financial assistance towards churches and chapels in England and Wales which might otherwise have found it extremely difficult to survive at all. Since its establishment in 1957 it has distributed grants to about 100 churches.

Legislation

PASTORAL MEASURE 1968, a legislative enactment of the former National Assembly of the Church of England, has as its principal object 'to provide for the better cure of souls', largely by a re-organization of parishes and by a more effective redeployment of the clergy. It also ensures that churches no longer required for parochial worship should be considered on their architectural and historic merits, before decisions are taken as to whether they should be demolished, put to alternative uses, or preserved.

DECLARATION OF REDUNDANCY, a legal enactment passed by the Church Commissioners and approved by Her Majesty in Council. Until a Pastoral Scheme, emanating from a diocese, has been approved, an Anglican church, whether or not it has already been closed, remains technically in use.

DEMOLITION CERTIFICATE is issued by the Advisory Board for Redundant Churches if it considers that this would not be 'objectionable on architectural or historic grounds'. At the end of a waiting period of 1–3 years after the Declaration of Redundancy, if the church is not considered worthy of preservation by the Redundant Churches Fund and an alternative use is not forthcoming, it then has to be demolished.

INSPECTION OF CHURCHES MEASURE 1955 was a legislative enactment by which statutory provision was made for the regular inspection of every Anglican church at least once in five years, by a suitably qualified architect, approved by the Diocesan Advisory Committee.

FACULTY JURISDICTION MEASURE 1964 governs faculties, or licences, which are issued by the Chancellor of the diocese for repair work to the fabric of a church or changes in its furnishings or internal appearance. Sales of church treasures, for example Communion plate, armour, paintings, require the authority of a Faculty and the case has to be argued fully in the Consistory Court.

LOCAL AUTHORITIES (HISTORIC BUILDINGS) ACT 1962 made it possible for every local authority to assist by grant or loan towards the repair or maintenance of any building of merit in its area.

INTRODUCTION: STAVE OFF DECAY

by Roy Strong

Mark you the floor? that square and speckled stone
Which looks so firm and strong
Is Patience;

And the other black and grave, wherewith each one
Is checkered all along,
Humility.

The gentle rising, which on either hand
Leads to the quire above,
Is Confidence;

But the sweet cement, which in one sure band
Ties the whole frame, is Love
And Charity.

George Herbert, 'The Church Floor'

This book sets out to combine what are usually widely divergent approaches to church buildings. Such a synthesis is deliberate because the future of our churches and chapels lies in the coming together to mutual purpose of these very different viewpoints. Worshipper, visitor, archaeologist, antiquarian, art historian, architect, restorer, priest, social worker, performer – all these find their focus in the church building and its environs. The concern of such disparate facets of our society is, however, an inherent force for their preservation. Through such a wide net, stretched still wider by the 'extended Church' more of the population is touched in some way by the fabric of church buildings (even if they reject what the building represents) than would willingly admit or would be apparent from electoral rolls or numbers of communicants on Easter Day. Unlike the problems facing our great country houses those confronting our churches are lit by a beam of hope.

The problem of our parish churches and their future is an emergent one and therefore, with foresight and planning, can be met before it is too late. This is what this book sets out to do, to warn and to counsel. Unlike country houses there is no appalling roll call of the departed, nor do churches – mercifully – attract an emotional reaction born of class conflict. In this sense, in spite of the continued decline in belief, their future is more assured in that their roots lie in the community around them. Rarely, however, is enough made of this potential. Pevsner's monumental *Buildings of England*, superb though it is, has encouraged an attitude to churches similar to that adopted in guides to hotels, a star system which notches up the art historical score regardless of the real significance of the church in relation to the other buildings around. Our way of looking at churches for a start needs to cut through this and be extended horizontally. They are without exception the creation of their own congregations in a way that the manor house never was. But this is only rarely brought out in guides to churches with their plans and shaded areas of Early English, Decorated or Perpendicular. Seldom are we ever given a glimpse of the building as the historic microcosm over the centuries of a community. Their very fabric tells us of prosperity and depression, of war and peace; extensions in size reflect rise in population; the names on headstones reveal the families who for generations moulded the life pattern of the land around. We need to develop for a wider public our approach to churches as expressions of past human beings, everyone's ancestors over the centuries, and shift from the crudity of categorizing a building on its aesthetic merits alone, ignoring all else.

Anyone interested in churches quickly becomes astounded by how little we really know about them. Although art history has been established as a discipline, for better or worse, in most of the universities in this country, where are the historians of British art? The study of British funerary sculpture is still in its infancy, much still unrecorded, and practically no attempt has been made to unravel its iconography, nor study the very important regional variations. Where are the studies of Victorian tiles, once cursed but now revealed as one of the nineteenth century's most pleasing additions to our churches? Research into decorative iron-work, into post-Reformation stained glass, into Victorian ecclesiastical textiles and embroidery, these are but a few of the fields awaiting serious exploration. For too long art has been foreign and the exhumation of yet another deplorable Italian Baroque master has been exulted above the study of our own heritage. And over all there is the art historians' disdain for the decorative arts as somehow an inferior area of study.

We need to shift our attitudes. Just as the Oxford Movement was obsessed by the hallowed stones and the beauty of holiness in an inevitable reaction against the casual approach of the Enlightenment, we, in the last quarter of the twentieth century, need to reformulate our own views. We are faced not only with declining belief (which, of course, could be reversed but such a reversal could or could not affect church buildings) but outright redundancy and demolition. Not only do we need to explore every avenue of alternative use – hall, museum exhibition space, theatre, offices, community centre – but think quite radically about our attitudes to the buildings which are still operable.

Poverty is a great preserver and inflation and recession will come as oddly welcome guests to those who dread the hand of the Restorer with his irresistible package of all things bright and beautiful. 'Stave off decay by daily care,' wrote William Morris almost a century ago. What marvellous wisdom Morris had and would that his sage words were more widely adhered to! But in thousands of churches, large and small, grand and humble, they are. The debt we owe to numberless ordinary people who sweep and wash floors, polish plate, wax woodwork or tend the graveyard is inestimable. The future of our parish churches belongs to that gloriously British eccentricity, the determination of the few. In the face of philistine authority a voice will raise itself, the cohorts will rally, and the impossible will be achieved. When it comes to the crunch, despair is not a British characteristic. And hundreds of churches which have been preserved and saved owe their existence to the inspired madness of the dedicated. To unsung loving hands and the forceful will of the few belongs the survival of the community's greatest visual expression of itself across the centuries.

8 November 1976

PART ONE
LEGACY & LOSS

ENGLAND: LEGACY
by Peter Burman

'For all the rustic beauty and historical attraction of those ancient fields and halls, one other feature of the man-made landscape focuses most of our attention and captures most of our imagination, the flint-grey parish church, often solitary away from the farmsteads, surrounded only by the fields. It provides the essential bearings in the detailed settlement-pattern, the nub of the local story.

'There are just on five hundred mediaeval churches standing in Suffolk; and, as we shall see, there were once about fifty more. Half a thousand represents a high concentration, for in all England there are reckoned to be about twelve thousand surviving mediaeval churches. Yet Suffolk scarcely seems congested with them. Her landscape is wide enough, and folded enough to hold them unobtrusively; and some of them are quite small . . .' Norman Scarfe The Suffolk Landscape *London 1972*

East Anglia is a remarkable part of the country for churches, and in writing about our legacy of church architecture and furnishings it is understandable if that part of England comes most readily to mind. The landscape here, though much more varied than those who do not know it might suppose, is dotted with churches so that to drive away from one is almost immediately to be confronted with another – and from some church towers, so it is said, fifty or sixty towers of other churches may be seen. In both Suffolk and Norfolk there are, too, more mediaeval churches than still survive intact: in Norfolk, which is the larger county, there are said not only to be 659 pre-1700 churches still surviving but, at the most recent and reliable count, about 249 ruined churches – in other words in Norfolk, which was known as 'Our Lady's Garden' (England was 'Our Lady's Dowry') in the Middle Ages, there were approaching 900 churches. Nor must we forget the churches of post-1700 date: there is Robert Adam's Gunton of 1769, for example, and the immensely

endearing church at Booton (*c.* 1875–91), designed by the Squarson, the Revd Whitwell Elwin, of which Lutyens said 'Very naughty, but built in the right spirit'. In their contents, of liturgical and historical significance, the churches of East Anglia are also especially remarkable: in Suffolk, for example, there is the rare 'Doom' of *c.* 1520 at Wenhaston, the fourteenth-century retable in the thatched church of Thornham Parva reached across a field, and (formerly part of an eighteenth-century reredos) at Bridgeham in Norfolk there are the painted figures of Moses and Aaron, of exceptional vividness and quality, the figure of Moses looking, in Pevsner's words, 'like a rustic version of El Greco'.

These examples could be multiplied a thousand-fold, and we have not yet considered the towns. Norwich has its great Norman cathedral and thirty-two mediaeval parish churches, and also many churches of later periods and other denominations – the Old Meeting in Colegate of 1693, the Octagon Chapel of 1754–6, and the Roman Catholic church of St John by George Gilbert Scott Junior and John Oldrid Scott, 1884–1910. (This church is built on such a scale and is of such magnificence that many visiting Norwich for the first time have mistaken it for the cathedral, and now it has indeed recently become the cathedral for the new Roman Catholic diocese of East Anglia.) In Suffolk, the mediaeval parish churches of Ipswich once numbered at least fifteen, of which twelve survive; in Bury St Edmunds the vast Abbey Church, now vanished except for a fragment of the west front and sundry other traces, was encompassed by three stately parish churches of which one, St James (with a noble crossing and choir by Stephen Dykes-Bower), is now the cathedral. St Mary's lies to the south of it with one of the most moving and beautiful churchyards in all England, and is celebrated as the burial place of Mary Tudor, sister

1. Cerne Abbas, Dorset; St Mary. A strong element in a rural landscape, and the focal point of its village

2. Exeter, Devon; St Michael. Rhode Hawkins 1867. The spire dominates the urban skyline

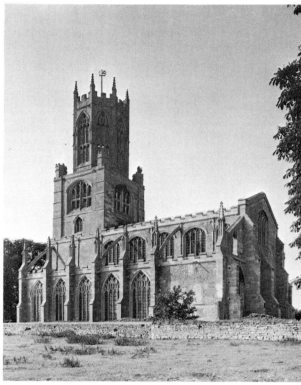

3. Fotheringhay, Northamptonshire; St Mary and All Saints. A magnificent former collegiate church, though lacking its choir which was demolished in 1573

4. Walpole, Suffolk. An early Dissenting chapel of 1647 formed out of two cottages with seventeenth-century furnishings

5. Stragglethorpe, Lincolnshire; St Michael. Untouched by major nineteenth-century restorations, this relatively modest church has a splendid Baroque monument to Richard Earle (d. 1697) by Thomas Green of Camberwell

6. Ipswich, Suffolk; Unitarian Church. The best surviving Nonconformist interior of its date, 1699–1700

8. Upmarden, West Sussex; St Michael. A marvellously unspoiled church, preserving thirteenth-century lancets unaltered and mediaeval floor. The nineteenth-century pulpit fits in well.

7. Southease, East Sussex. A large Norman church with later windows inserted. One of the only three round towers of Sussex. The textures of flint walls and handmade tiles are especially attractive.

9. Upleadon, Gloucestershire; St Mary. Splendid timber-framed tower of *c.* 1500

10. Duntisbourne Rous, Gloucestershire; St Michael. Saxon church in the Cotswolds, below the chancel is a small crypt chapel

of Henry VIII and wife of Henry Brandon, Duke of Suffolk. The third church has disappeared altogether. In Bury there is also a Baroque Unitarian Chapel of 1711, with brickwork of the finest quality, and a delightful Roman Catholic church of Grecian style and relatively early date (1837) in which secular furnishings from the demolished Rushbrooke Hall have been used to good effect.

Turning to interiors and furnishings, there are in Norfolk painted screens of uncommon quality such as those, deservedly well-known, at Ranworth and Barton Turf; there is a carved wooden font canopy at Trunch, more like a baldacchino than what we ordinarily understand by a 'canopy'; there are the great roofs, like that at Cawston; and there is the extraordinary atmosphere of so many of them, speaking of a continuity of worship, of village life and village burial, of an ability to survive (if not quite intact still remarkably rich) many a political upheaval in the country as a whole. Perhaps the most memorable of all, though everyone will have his favourite, is Salle: a ticking clock in the seventeenth-century tower gallery seems to measure out time, but otherwise this vast church in a tiny hamlet appears to have been immune from the passage of the centuries. At the same time it has managed to collect something fine from almost all of them: mediaeval stained glass, the seventeenth-century woodwork, monuments and ledger slabs of the seventeenth and eighteenth centuries, a made-up triple-decker pulpit, and so on. A poem in *The Ancient People*, by Glen Cavaliero, catches it exactly:

'*It rides the fields, superb, above decay;*
ashen with age, its door will open
on to an emptiness so huge
it could let in the sky,
and so bright that prayers go blind
in the cold glare of its appalling day . . .'

Suffolk boasts one of the oldest Nonconformist chapels in England – the Congregational Chapel at Walpole, near Halesworth, built as a cottage in 1607 and adapted for use as a chapel as early as 1647. The furnishings inside are all wooden – galleries, seats, double-decker pulpit, rails, hat-pegs and the like. It is an astonishing survival from the ethos of an earlier time.

Other remarkable survivals include such treasures as the *Ranworth Antiphonal*, at Ranworth in Norfolk, a mediaeval service book in its original home; the sindon cloth (a cloth to cover the pyx, holding the reserved Blessed Sacrament) and burse (a case for the corporal, the cloth on which the Host lies during the Mass) survive from Hessett church in Suffolk, though sensibly on loan to the British Museum. In the same church there is also much mediaeval

glass, and wall-paintings of St Barbara, the Seven Deadly Sins, and Christ of the Trades. Both counties are rich in stained glass and wall-paintings. At Redgrave, also in Suffolk, are two particularly fine monuments – that to Sir Nicholas Bacon, Lord Keeper to Elizabeth I, carved by the master sculptor of the reign of James I, Nicholas Stone, and the masterpiece of Thomas Green of Camberwell, the monument to Sir John Holt, Lord Chief Justice of England for twenty-one years. *d.* 1710, with a large central seated figure and groups of *putti* on the cornice. These two monuments represent different aspects of the Baroque style in England, an earlier (the Bacon monument was made in 1616) and a later; the hall has been demolished so that, without them, there would be no tangible sign of the exalted personages who lived in this obscure village.

Probably no other counties have so much to offer the mediaevalist as these, with more than 1,100 pre-1700 churches between them. But Lincolnshire has also a notable inheritance of churches, ranging from the Saxon west-work at St Peter, Barton upon Humber, the Norman work at Stow (where the chancel was without stone vaulting until Pearson triumphantly completed it in the nineteenth century), the thirteenth-century lead-covered spire at Long Sutton, recently repaired, and the Decorated splendour of Heckington to the Georgian elegance and completeness of Langton by Spilsby and such nineteenth-century treasures as the little church of Cold Hanworth (designed by a little-known architect, John Croft of Islington, 1863), alone except for its neighbouring farm, and the Newland Congregational Chapel in Lincoln, which was paid for largely by the local engineering firm, Ruston & Hornsby, and contains an exuberance of cast-iron ornamentation which would do credit to the finest of the main London rail termini.

Devonshire and Somerset are also counties where important churches lie thick upon the ground. In Devon there is a recognizable West Country plan, with three equal aisles closely akin to the continental 'hall church' type. Somerset has a famous series of towers, mostly dating from the late mediaeval period and of a stateliness scarcely to be paralleled in any other part of England. Both Devon and Somerset have an astonishing amount of mediaeval woodwork surviving, and together with Cornwall they were also early strongholds of dissenting congregations so that there are Nonconformist buildings like the Come to Good Friends' Meeting House of 1710 near Calstock in Cornwall, and in Somerset the Rook Lane Congregational Chapel (now redundant) in Frome of 1707, and the handsome Meeting House at Long Sutton

11. Didmarton, Gloucestershire; St Michael. A mediaeval church with eighteenth-century fittings

12. Locko Park Chapel, Derbyshire. 1669. Sumptuous Victorian remodelling of a seventeenth-century chapel

13. Ingestre, Staffordshire; St Mary. Sir Christopher Wren, 1676. Although remote from London, the design and craftsmanship are of the calibre of Wren's city churches

14. Shobdon, Hertfordshire; St John the Evangelist. 1752–6. Rococo Gothic at its most elegant and fanciful

15. Great Packington, Warwickshire; St James. Joseph Bonomi, 1789–90. One of the most powerful of all English Neoclassical churches

16. East Lulworth, Dorset; St Mary. John Tasker, 1786–7. A pre-Emancipation Act Roman Catholic church on a cloverleaf plan in the grounds of the great house, its ecclesiastical purpose subtly underplayed

17. Ranmore, Surrey; St Bartholomew. Sir Gilbert Scott, 1859, at his most impressive as a designer

18. Fimber, Yorkshire; St Mary. 1871. Street's chancel retains its splendid fittings intact

19. Colehill, Dorset; St Michael. W. D. Caröe, 1893–5, an Arts and Crafts architect of great ability and inventiveness

dating from 1717. In Bristol, where there is a super-abundance of churches of all denominations, there is a concentration of churches in the historic centre which can only be rivalled by London, York, Norwich and Ipswich. It seems, incidentally, to be a peculiarly English trait – the proliferation of small city churches with exiguous parishes, probably representing the extent of tenement holdings or other significant land-holding patterns. London, at the time of the Great Fire in 1666, had 106 parish churches within the City walls. A town as small as Shaftesbury in Dorset had twelve mediaeval parish churches where now there is only one, and the royal patronage of Wilton in Wiltshire probably accounted for a similar number with magnificent monastic foundations in both these towns in addition. Mention of the monastic churches may remind us of that relatively small number of former monastic churches which have happily survived as magnificent parish churches, albeit for the most part truncated like Leominster (Herefordshire), Binham (Norfolk) and Malmesbury (Wiltshire). Bolton Abbey, in Yorkshire, is a particularly striking example: the nave survives as the parish church and the crossing, transepts, and choir as impressive ruins. The county of Dorset has no less than three of the more spectacular instances of monastic survival churches in Christchurch Priory, Milton Abbey and Sherborne Abbey; Milton Abbey survived virtually as the chapel of the great house, now a school, and is among the tiny handful of Anglican churches which belong to Trustees.

Derbyshire is a county where the visitor avid for mediaeval churches might not immediately think of spending a few days. Yet he would be richly rewarded by churches such as Repton, with its extensive Saxon work, by the Norman grandeur of Melborne, by Tissington in its harmonious feudal village setting, by Tideswell, 'cathedral of the Peaks', and others. County Durham, another unfashionable county in this context, can show the Saxon to perfection in Escomb and in the stately late mediaeval church of Brancepeth are the Gothic Survival (or Revival?) post-Restoration screens and stalls, and font cover, given by Bishop Cosin. Lancashire has such fine mediaeval churches as Ormskirk, Lancaster St Mary, and Sefton. Leicestershire and Northamptonshire are both counties which had readily available supplies of good building stone, and where there scarcely seems to be a village without a mediaeval parish church. Warwickshire and Worcestershire churches tend to be relatively modest, though there were three mediaeval churches on a grand scale in Coventry and the great parish churches of Holy Trinity, Stratford-upon-Avon, and St Mary, Warwick,

are notable. In the western counties of the Midlands and Welsh border timber-framing was used as extensively in churches as in secular buildings, and produced such remarkable structures as Upleadon in Gloucestershire, Lower Peover, Cheshire, and the detached belfry at Pembridge, Herefordshire. Timber-framing is also common in Essex, where there is a whole series of spectacular timber-framed steeples, like those at Blackmore and West Hanningfield and (on a more modest scale) at Mundon. In counties like Essex where stone of any description was difficult to come by, and expensive to import, it is not surprising that the use of brick in church building was adopted, producing such superb results as at East Horndon or the west tower at Ingatestone.

In considering our post-mediaeval heritage there is, as much as before the Civil War, an embarrassment of riches. In the three quarters of a century or so after the Reformation there was little need or impetus for new church building, though there was a good deal of 'liturgical re-ordering'. Of this concern for the adaptation of mediaeval churches for a plainly spoken vernacular liturgy the most frequently encountered tangible survivals are the Elizabethan Communion cups and the numerous and often very handsome Communion tables, Elizabethan or early Stuart. The Royal Arms were also introduced into churches and although most of the examples now to be seen date from the Hanoverian era, when there was presumably a drive to replace earlier ones with the symbol of a new dynasty, there are some early ones like the Royal Arms of Elizabeth I at Tivetshall St Margaret in Norfolk. The Arms of Charles I, Charles II and Queen Anne are sometimes found and – very rarely – of the two Jameses.

Most counties can show one or two specimens of relatively humble seventeenth-century churches, but it is in the towns that many of the best are to be found. For instance, in the heart of Leeds, the church of St John, provided by the wealthy John Harrison in 1632–4, is a building not only significant for its use of the Per-pendicular style about one hundred years after it began to go out of fashion but for its breathtaking wealth of original woodwork which includes the pews and a sumptuous screen across both nave and wide south aisle. Almost contemporary with it is St Katharine Creechurch in the City of London, consecrated in 1616 by Archbishop Laud (the ceremonial used was amongst the charges laid against him at his trial). The churches by Wren in the City of London are too well-known to require singling out, but less well-known is Ingestre in Staffordshire, built in 1676 for Walter Chetwynd, a fellow member with Wren of the Royal Society and almost certainly by him.

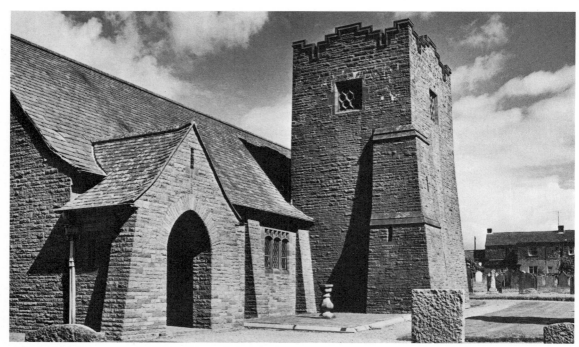

20. Plympton Wall, Cumbria, St John the Evangelist. Sir Robert Lorimer, 1907. A clever fusion of the Voysey-domestic with the Scottish vernacular style

21. Kegworth, Leicestershire; St Andrew. A stately fourteenth-century church. Over the chancel arch an uncommonly fine Royal Arms of Charles II dated 1684

22. Trunch, Norfolk; St Botolph. The font cover, a magnificent specimen of mediaeval woodcarving

23. Ottery, Devon; St Mary. Font by William Butterfield, who restored the church *c.* 1850

24. Blue Idol, Sussex; Friends Meeting House. Converted out of one wing of a half-timbered cottage for William Penn in 1691

25. Chesterfield, Derbyshire; Unitarian Chapel. Classical quoins and vernacular mullioned windows. The graveyard is a valuable survival – many Nonconformist congregations made efforts to provide their own burial grounds, but they are often forgotten and neglected

26. Little Walsingham, Norfolk; Methodist Chapel. 1793–4. Elegance with a minimum of detail

27. Buckingham Gate, London; Westminster Methodist Chapel. F. W. Poulton, 1864–5. The architecture of High Victorian Nonconformity at its most spectacular

One of Wren's closest and ablest associates, Nicholas Hawksmoor, designed the tower of St Michael-upon-Cornhill in the City and, following the passing of the Act for the Building of Fifty New Churches in 1712, created a strange and original series of powerful and haunting masterpieces – St Alphege, Greenwich, St George, Bloomsbury, St Mary Woolnoth, City, Christ Church, Spitalfields, St George-in-the-East, Stepney, and St Anne, Limehouse. At much the same time James Gibbs and Thomas Archer were building their own Baroque masterpieces – Gibbs' St Mary le Strand was also designed for the Commission for Fifty New Churches, while St Martin-in-the-Fields was built at the charge of the parish, whose parshioners included the reigning sovereign. Thomas Archer built St John, Smith Square, Westminster, and St Paul, Deptford, for the Commission, and in Birmingham he built the less ebullient but still handsome church of St Philip, now the Anglican cathedral.

Throughout the eighteenth century, and indeed throughout the nineteenth, families of the nobility and of the landed gentry repaired or rebuilt the churches on their estates or financed the building of completely new churches. There is a delightful group of such churches in Leicestershire and Rutland, of which perhaps the most enjoyable are Stapleford (which is classical, and in the environs of the great house) and Kings Norton (which is Gothic, and superbly sited in the rolling landscape). There is also a rather special category of churches which were built as elements in a 'designed landscape', part of the private Elysium which is the *raison d'être* of the eighteenth-century landscape park. Gunton, in Norfolk, could be mistaken for a temple any day, and Robert Adam also designed the furnishings for Croome D'Abitot in Worcestershire, to complement the church designed and cunningly sited by none other than 'Capability' Brown.

As one contemplates the church building of the nineteenth century, two features present themselves as being particularly obvious and striking. The first is the prodigious number of churches and chapels which were built, for this is of course the era not only of Anglican revival – both Catholic and Evangelical – but the period of expansion and self-confidence amongst the Nonconformist denominations. The growing cities of the north of England and of the Midlands were, moreover, centres of dissent as well as of industrial prosperity. In Halifax there were two rival families, the Crossleys and the Akroyds, who were Congregationalist and Anglican respectively.

For the Congregationalists Sir Francis Crossley built Square Congregational Church, designed by Joseph James, 1855–7, with a spire of *c.* 235 feet in the Decorated style, seen to perfection from the great cobbled square of the 1775 Piece Hall. Looking from the same spot to the north, through the entrance archway of the Piece Hall, can be seen a distant view of the no less spectacular spire of All Souls, Haley Hill, designed by Sir Gilbert Scott (who described it as 'on the whole, my best church') for Col. Akroyd, as the functional and visual climax of his model housing estate, Akroyden. Begun in 1856, it is hard to resist the idea that emulation of Sir Francis Crossley was a contributory factor.

The second immediately observable factor is that so many of the very best architects of the High Victorian and Late Victorian periods were principally church architects, or their churches are among their finest and most memorable buildings. Coupled with this is the relative obscurity of many of the architects employed by Roman Catholics and Nonconformists – as witness the choice of Joseph James and Sir Gilbert Scott, respectively, in Halifax. The Emancipation of Roman Catholics did not take place until 1829, before which the freedom to erect or maintain openly places where the Mass could be said was severely circumscribed. The reputation of Pugin is well established, but other Roman Catholic architects are only now emerging as significant figures – among them Joseph Aloysius Hansom, the architect of St Walburge, Preston, 1850–54, whose firm was also later responsible for such outstanding buildings as the Roman Catholic cathedral of St Philip Neri, Arundel, 1868–9, and Our Lady and the English Martyrs, Cambridge, 1887–90.

Relatively few architects seem to have crossed the denominational barriers until the twentieth century, and seldom even then – an interesting comment on the operation of patronage. But the 'movements' which have influenced architecture generally in England – the Arts and Crafts Movement, the 'Modern Movement' and so on – have exercised their influence dispassionately. The Church is still a great patron of architecture and the arts, though the post Second World War church architecture – owing no doubt chiefly to the shortage of funds – has not been of the imaginative and artistic level of that, say, in Germany and Switzerland (where the funding of church work, both for repairs and for new building, is on a generous scale) but the commissioning of minor artefacts for worship has often produced works of distinction.

ENGLAND: LOSS
by Marcus Binney

Closure, abandonment and demolition threaten churches and chapels of all denominations on an alarming scale. In 1960 the Bridges Report estimated that some 790 Church of England churches would become redundant in the following fifteen to twenty years. Following the recommendations of the report a statutory procedure was set up for dealing with redundant churches in 1968 by the Pastoral Measure. By 1 November 1976, 592 churches had been declared redundant, and of the 472 cases dealt with 153 had been or were to be demolished, including some twenty-three buildings officially listed as of special architectural or historic interest. In its Annual Report for 1975 the Advisory Board for Redundant Churches forecast that 'by 1980 over 1,000 churches will probably have been declared redundant and that thereafter the redundancy rate will either be maintained or increased as the result of inflation and the redeployment of the clergy'.

Redundancy among the Free Churches has been even more marked. In 1974, according to the statistics kept by the Registrar-General, 331 non-Anglican places of worship in England and Wales were closed. In 1975 the figure was 345. The Methodists have closed some 5,000 chapels in the last forty years and in the autumn of 1976 more than 200 of the 2,200 United Reformed churches were for sale. According to the researches of Mr Christopher Stell, who is preparing a definitive volume on Nonconformist chapels for the Royal Commission on Historical Monuments, only one in five of the 3,701 chapels and meeting houses existing in 1801 now remain, and of these eighty have gone since 1940. Of those built before 1850 no less than 400, either listed or of listable quality, have been demolished since then. Unless positive steps are taken there is a real danger that the second half of the twentieth century will be remembered as an age of destruction of religious art and architecture comparable to the ravages of the Reformation and the Civil War, the neglect of the eighteenth century and the too-ready hand of the Victorian restorer.

One of the most controversial of the 1950s losses was St Nicholas, Colchester, by Sir George Gilbert Scott, a proud work in a prominent position in the middle of the town. This was ignominiously demolished to make way for a supermarket. Shortly after came the demolition of the largely Saxon church of St Peter the Less in Chichester. Since 1968 the most deplorable Church of England losses have included St Paul's, Penge, the interior of which was covered with stencilling of almost fluorescent brilliance; The Saviour, in Bolton, Lancashire, listed Grade A; St Peter's, Rochester, a highly individual church with three cross gables and a porch with a saddleback roof. Among Nonconformist chapels a most disturbing loss was the handsome early-seventeenth-century Unitarian chapel at Crediton, complete with all its woodwork, and a building of sufficient quality to have been taken into guardianship by the Department of the Environment. An equal tragedy was the demolition of the majestic Scottish Presbyterian Church in Regent Square, which had a twin-towered façade inspired by York Minster. Disgraceful too was the demolition of the delightful octagonal Regency chapel at Wisbech, one of only four octagonally planned churches in England. By comparison losses among Roman Catholic churches have been far fewer, though the handsome Neo-classical chapel at Houghton, Yorkshire, went in 1959.

If relatively few buildings of the first rank have gone the number destroyed of churches by provincial architects of talent, and of buildings which gave character and identity to the towns in which they stood, has been alarming. Too often churches are evaluated primarily, if not wholly, according to their importance in the history of architectural development. The best and earliest examples of

28. Colchester, Essex; St Nicholas. Sir George Gilbert Scott 1875–6. Demolished in 1955 to make way for a supermarket

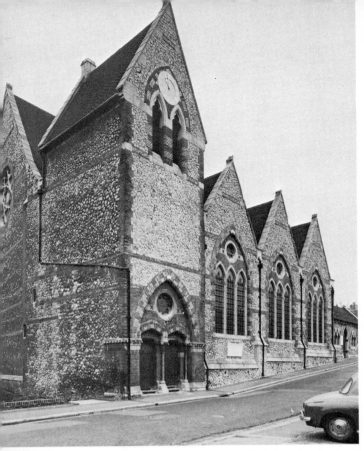

29. Rochester, Kent; St Peter. Ewan Christian, 1858–60. One of Christian's best churches

30. Penge, Kent; St Paul. Bassett Keeling 1865, with painted decoration by Clayton and Bell. Demolition certificate issued July 1973 after only a year of redundancy

31. Bolton, Lancashire; The Saviour. Paley & Austin, 1882–5. Listed Grade A. Demolition certificate November 1974

32. Crediton, Devon; Unitarian Chapel. A major Nonconformist loss. Demolished

33. Crediton, Devon; Unitarian Chapel. The woodwork was intact

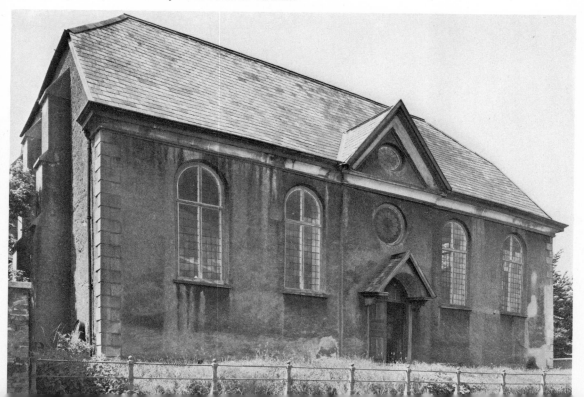

successive styles, the buildings of leading architects, are set above secondary or 'derivative' works which are considered as much-of-a-much-ness, to some extent interchangeable. Yet is is quite wrong to value most churches by a national yardstick: the majority are local assets, built and belonging to individual communities, which often possess no other building of comparable age, interest or merit. What appears a dim church to a committee man in London looking at an indifferent photograph taken on a dull day of a building he has never seen may be a key local landmark.

This process has not been helped by the tendency of architectural historians to judge all buildings by the standards of the best, against which others must be compared unfavourably. The most consistent offenders are the volumes of *The Buildings of England*. Here churches are not only often damned by faint praise but by the lack of any comment at all, and in some cases expressions such as 'a Gothic spire ill-suited to the neighbourhood' or 'the work of an ignorant goth' have been quoted to support the case for demolition.

34. Wisbech, Cambridgeshire; Octagon Chapel. William Swansborough, 1827–30. Demolished before 1970

A church is often the oldest building in the village or town it stands in: streets and houses are grouped around them giving them an importance far beyond their intrinsic merit as a structure. At Whitby a perfect natural site has been ruined by bad development. The church alone redeems the sprawl, and when it goes the waterfront will lose its main feature. In the same town the former Wesley Chapel in Church Street was a landmark simply by virtue of its elevated site, and the monumental steps leading up to it. St Michael's, Star Street, Paddington, though gutted in the war still gave a memorable note of drama to a pleasant but unremarkable street.

These examples of former churches making major contributions to the townscape can be multiplied up and down the country. The massive rock-faced St John the Evangelist, in Watlington, Reading, was given a demolition certificate in 1973. The full-blooded spire of St Paul's, Princes Park, in Liverpool, survived the destruction of the nave, only to follow soon after. The towering Baptist church of the Redeemer in Hagley Road, Birmingham, went in 1975. Many Nonconformist chapels are important guides to the work of thoroughly competent, if strictly secondary architects such as the Pritchetts of York and Darlington, the Habershons of London and Newport, Mawson and Lockwood and John Tarring. The range of types among nineteenth-century Nonconformist chapels extends from strict temple-form buildings to serious Gothic revival in competition with Anglican churches. Often, however, it is the more light-hearted essays that had the greatest appeal; that in Stockport Road, Manchester, has gone after suffering the ignominy of being converted into a motor showroom. At Launceston in Cornwall the former Baptist chapel was so engagingly frivolous that few would have guessed it was a church, and it would surely have made an excellent house.

Many Nonconformist chapels have hardly been touched since they were built and as a result retain their original woodwork and fittings intact. Alas this completeness has often not helped protect them; the Congregational church at Ebley, Stroud, with pews and galleries laid out on a semi-circular plan went about 1970; the Essex Unitarian Church in Kensington with an enormous amount of fine Arts and Crafts woodwork went in 1973; consent to demolish the Swindon Baptist Tabernacle was granted in 1975 – here a handsome temple form exterior contained an unusually elegant interior, with arcaded galleries supported by cast-iron columns with delicate leaf capitals.

The usual explanations given for demolitions of such churches – dwindling congregations and soaring costs of upkeep – conceal in my view the real and more disturbing reasons for their loss. There is first an unwillingness, sometimes amounting to a refusal, among some church-men to accept that fine architecture can be any kind of asset to worship or missionary work, a sad irony in an age in which agnostics as much as believers recognize the numinous qualities of churches. Indeed, there are some clergy and ministers who appear to harbour feelings towards old buildings of a vehemence that the Victorians reserved for the 'foul torrent of the Renaissance'. At Andover parishioners who raised money to repair the parish church were prevented by the vicar from carrying out the work until they won their way in the consistory court. At Tunbridge Wells, when local people sought to save Holy Trinity church from demolition, a local minister wrote to the newspaper saying it was 'a straight fight

36. Houghton Hall Chapel, Yorkshire. Roman Catholic chapel by Joseph Ireland. Demolished 1959

35. Regent Square, London; Scottish Presbyterian Church. 1825. Inspired by York Minster. Demolished c. 1955.

between christians and conservationists' when in fact many of those opposing the plan were churchgoers.

As John Harvey wrote in *Conservation of Buildings* (1968), 'Too many buildings are being sacrificed not to real necessity but to an expediency based on a false set of values. Old buildings, it is argued, are costly of upkeep: a modern replacement would greatly relieve the financial burden on the church.' The fact is that supposedly utilitarian churches have developed serious faults in twenty-five to thirty years and sometimes in five or ten, and have nothing like the life-expectancy of a strong building constructed of seasoned materials of a kind that can no longer be afforded: initial costs should not be confused with long-term ones. Moreover, the alarming figures quoted for repairing churches are usually the result of a failure to carry out ordinary maintenance. At a meeting of the Ecclesiastical Architects and Surveyors Association in 1975 one member suggested that 'perhaps

37. Whitby, Yorkshire; St Michael. J. B. & W. Atkinson, 1847–8. A landmark on the waterfront. Demolition certificate March 1976.

38. Whitby, Yorkshire; Wesley Chapel. A simple building given grandeur by its position. Demolished

39. Paddington, London; St Michael. Rhode Hawkins, 1860. A landmark in an otherwise unremarkable street. Demolished *c.* 1960

40. Reading, Berkshire; St John the Evangelist. W. A. Dixon, 1872–3. A spire dominating a whole neighbourhood. To be demolished when new church completed.

half of the major defects in churches are caused by such elementary neglects as not cleaning out the gutters'.

The desire to rationalize plant and manpower has led certain dioceses to draw up pastoral plans which threaten dozens of churches with closure: both Lincoln and Norwich have spoken of figures over 100. Yet in both these dioceses there are clergy who successfully minister to four and even five parishes. The fact is that some congregations, so far from being unwilling to continue, are being force-marched into redundancy against their will. St Saviour in Leeds not only has a strong core of regular attenders but an endowment fund sufficient to cover all costs of maintenance, yet this is threatened with closure. The parishioners of Christ Church, Brixton, had to take their case to the Privy Council to prevent the Diocese and the Church Commissioners from closing their church. More recently the congregation of St Mark's, Silvertown,

a magnificent Teulon church in Woolwich, have lost a determined struggle to keep their church open.

Of course there are cases where attendances are so minimal as to make closure quite inevitable. But here postwar planning policies, which have been carried out with such ruthless zeal by local authorities, have much to answer for. The centres of cities like Leeds and Liverpool have been depopulated by planners just as surely as the Highlands were cleared by the lairds. In Liverpool the inner city population has fallen from 600,000 in 1931 to 290,000 in 1971: large areas of the inner city have been flattened, leaving churches in deserts of wasteland a target for vandals and an invitation to arson. The tragic – and predictable – gutting of St Clement's Sheepscar in Leeds within weeks of closure is a case in point.

Churches, particularly in the country, may be the subject of deep, if unarticulated feelings and attachments. Studies

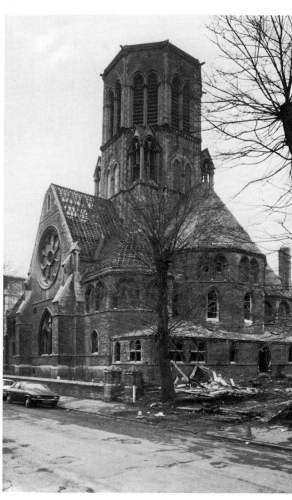

41. Princes Park, Liverpool; St Paul. A. H. Holme, 1846–8. A soaring spire. Demolished January 1975.

42. Birmingham; Baptist Church of the Redeemer. Demolished 1975.

43. Manchester; Former Congregational Chapel. Demolished after the ignominy of conversion into a car show room

44. Southwark, London; Baptist Chapel. The interior

45. Southwark, London; Baptist Chapel. 1863–4. A temple-form chapel. Demolished *c.* 1970

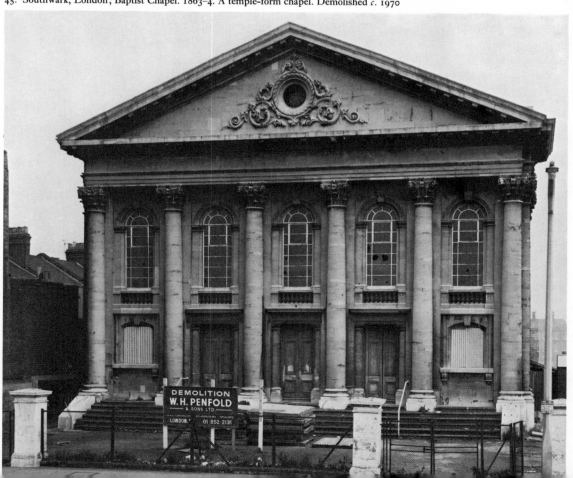

46. Ebley, Stroud, Gloucestershire; Congregational Church. 1880–81. Demolished *c.* 1970

47. Launceston, Cornwall; Baptist Chapel. Late eighteenth century. Demolished by 1969

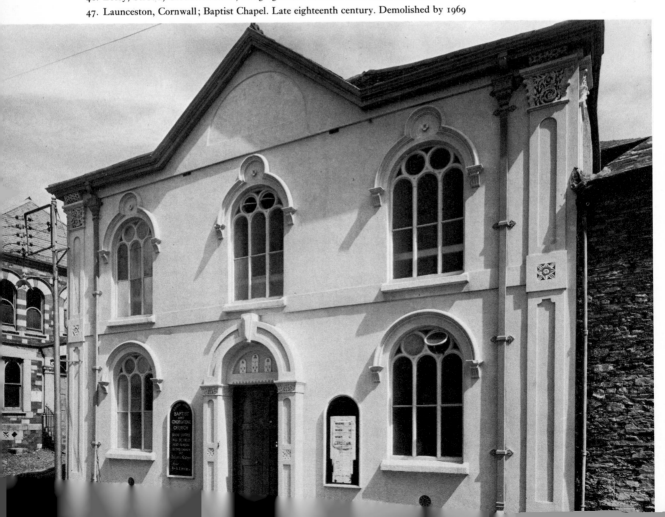

by the Grubb Institute of Behavioural Studies have shown that a community which is deprived of its church feels that it has been devalued, and community life is itself weakened. In a letter to the *Times* the Institute's project director wrote that when people hear 'of clergy recommending that churches should be closed or demolished or allowed to fall into disrepair they feel the clergy have now lost confidence in the Christian faith'. The worth of a church therefore should not be measured by Sunday attendances: many people relate to the church by knowing that a member of the family or a leader of the community attends church as it were on their behalf. Others relate even more vicariously, relying on their knowledge that the church is there, and turning to it in times of stress.

Too many church demolitions have been both senseless and needless: could not a simple building like Old Woodhall, with its pretty waisted spire and spirelets, have been left peacefully standing in its unkempt churchyard? A simple small church like West Milton in Dorset could surely have become a house. Quite a proportion of the churches and chapels demolished have been in very sound condition, and readily adaptable to new uses. Examples are Christ Church, Knottingley, Yorkshire and the aptly named Mint Methodist Chapel in Exeter.

Under the provisions of the Pastoral Measure a Church of England church can be peremptorily demolished if the Advisory Board for Redundant Churches certify that it is 'of such small architectural and historic merit that demolition would not be objectionable on that score' – without any chance being allowed for a search for a new use. The tragedy is that well-built relatively recent churches likely to be demolished under this provision have a greater chance of finding a new use than more historic ones, and if an opportunity was allowed, they would help demonstrate that conversion is both practical and economic.

The pioneers here are the Sports Councils. Finding that new sports centres were too expensive in present financial circumstances they are looking for existing buildings of all kinds to convert for sports purposes – drill halls, railway stations, warehouses and churches. For chapels and churches often have the open floor space and high ceilings required for popular indoor sports such as badminton, five-a-side football, squash and gymnastics. The need now is to persuade local authorities to convert churches to other community purposes for which public money is available such as libraries, community centres and arts centres. Every time a local authority sanctions a new building for one of these purposes, it is condemning one of the historic buildings it is charged with protecting. A proposal to turn

48. Leeds; St Clement Sheepscar. Severely damaged by arson soon after it was closed. Demolished 1976

the mediaeval church of St Lawrence, Evesham, into the town's public library was turned down because the county secretary reported that 'the building though accepted as an architectural and historical treasure is perhaps not in keeping with the concept of a modern public library service'. If this is the case, one asks, why does the Saxon church of St Peter in the East, Oxford, make such an excellent library for St Edmund Hall?

What is needed is a much more imaginative and flexible approach to the future use of churches. In many inner-city areas there is an acute lack of provision for children to play. Here unwanted churches could become day nurseries, indoor recreation areas and crèches. In the country some could serve as refuges for hikers and holidaymakers.

49. Kensington, London; Essex Unitarian Chapel. 1887. A remarkable interior. Demolished 1973

50. Swindon, Wiltshire; Baptist Tabernacle. W. H. Read, 1886. Permission to demolish granted 1975

51. Birkenhead, Cheshire; Holy Trinity. Cunningham and Holme, 1837–40. Demolished

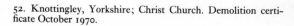

52. Knottingley, Yorkshire; Christ Church. Demolition certificate October 1970.

53. Old Woodhall, Lincolnshire; St Margaret. Demolition certificate July 1972

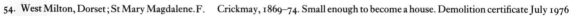

54. West Milton, Dorset; St Mary Magdalene. F. Crickmay, 1869–74. Small enough to become a house. Demolition certificate July 1976

Redundant churches and chapels are too often seen as a problem: instead, they could be regarded as an opportunity to meet urgent community needs for which new buildings will often be unavailable.

Finally, it should be asked whether more churches could be given a new lease of life by being handed over to other denominations, particularly non-Christian ones which are often looking for places of worship in the very areas where redundancies occur. In Spitalfields, a former Huguenot church is now a mosque, but the Church of England Synod was swayed against this form of disposal following an impassioned plea by an ex-Hindu convert. Yet is it right to use one's property and heritage to make life more difficult for other religions and does it not conflict with the basic principle of freedom of worship which Christians accept?

55. Exeter, Devon; The Mint Methodist Chapel. 1812. Well-maintained and adaptable to a new use. Demolished *c.* 1968

56. Barton under Needwood, Staffordshire; Primitive Methodist Chapel, 1842. Demolished *c.* 1970

SCOTLAND
by Colin McWilliam

No visitor can spend much time north of the border without noticing that churches have a special place in the Scottish scene and in Scottish history. With such a history, change has been of the essence. As to decay and redundancy, one might reasonably guess that half Scotland's churches have no future in their proper role. This is not just because there are fewer church-goers. There are also historical reasons in the shape of nineteenth-century divisions and twentieth-century unions.

Against this background, the task is to look at Scottish churches and what has happened to them; to consider how their future prospects answer the need to preserve them as works of art; and where these prospects fall short, to see what might be done.

The largest denomination is the established Church of Scotland. It dates from the first National Covenant of the Reformed Faith (1557), followed by the final break with Rome (1560) which can be said to mark the Scottish Reformation. John Knox and Andrew Melville, authors of the first and the second *Book of Discipline*, were its founder and builder. Bishops made their first exit in 1596, their final one in 1690. One of the Church's best loved institutions, the Metrical Psalms, have their origin in the *Westminster Confession of Faith* (1645).

The Reformed Church used the mediaeval buildings it had inherited. Change and decay show themselves together from the start. Unlike many of their brother reformers on the continent, or the more flexible Church of England, the Scots had no use for multi-cell buildings. They wanted a single space in which to hear the Word of God and to share the Lord's Supper at their long communion tables (these persisted right into the nine-

teenth century in many churches, and can still be seen, for example, at Durisdeer in Dumfriesshire). For the cathedrals and other great churches there were two possibilities; either the use of one part as a parish church and the neglect of the rest, or subdivision into separate churches for the use of different congregations. The latter fate befell many of the burgh kirks which were the

58. Glasgow; St Mungo's Cathedral. The choir screen. The mediaeval cathedral is the property of the Crown

57. Kirkwall, Orkney; St Magnus's Cathedral. A mediaeval cathedral which still bears this title although used for Church of Scotland worship. Property of the local authority

grandest late mediaeval churches in Scotland. Later restoration subsequently reversed these changes, for instance by building up the abandoned sections of Brechin and Dunblane Cathedrals, or by re-uniting the interiors of burgh kirks like that of St Giles in Edinburgh. Those at Dundee and Aberdeen are still divided, though largely rebuilt.

Smaller churches were easier to adapt, the more so because after the Norman period the elaborate parish church was the exception rather than the rule in mediaeval Scotland; for such exceptions there is always a reason such as an original collegiate foundation (e.g. Dalkeith and St Monance) or a special benefaction. Until the mid-nineteenth century only one sort of compartmentation was countenanced in a reformed church – the division of the seating, with special lofts or galleries for the incorporated tradesmen whose status grew throughout the seventeenth century, or for the families of local landowners whose

burial vaults were often sited beneath their gallery. Two of the best surviving 'lairds' lofts' are at Kilbirnie, Ayrshire (1642) and Abercorn, Lothian (c. 1700).

One of the first purpose-built reformed churches is at Burntisland in Fife (1592), a curious square building with a central tower and trades' lofts all complete. The early seventeenth century produced one or two backward-looking designs like the Kirk of the Greyfriars in Edinburgh (1612), and some notable hybrids like Archbishop Spottiswoode's English Gothic church at Dairsie, Fife (1621; now a book store for a department of St Andrew's University), and Edinburgh's Tron Kirk (1637). This lost a limb of its T plan in the late eighteenth century and its Netherlandish belfry in 1824 (the Dutch connection is more often seen in interior woodwork), but it survived to be bought by a developer who, incredibly, was handsomely compensated in 1963 for not being allowed to demolish it. This is a case in which a historic church also

59. Edinburgh; Tron Kirk. John Mylne, 1637. The steeple a replacement by R. & R. Dickson 1828. Now in the course of restoration by Edinburgh District Council but no use has yet been decided for the brutally gutted interior

60. Cromarty; East Parish Church. Anderson Monument, 1704, with *memento mori*

happened to be a popular institution, so there was action. The Secretary of State for Scotland later bought it back for the City of Edinburgh which has restored the shell but gutted the interior for a purpose as yet unknown.

After church building burgeoned in the early seventeenth century one main type, a much humbler one, prevailed for the next 200 years. It is a plain rectangular box, sometimes built on the foundations of a mediaeval church, its harled (i.e. rough-rendered) walls seldom enriched by anything more than a birdcage belfry on one of its crowstepped gables, or perhaps a moulded doorway or a sundial. The galleried ends have two-storey fenestration, and a blank section of wall half way along one side, flanked by tall windows, shows the location of the pulpit. There is often a further limb (or in the Scots sense a jamb or aisle) facing the pulpit and making the plan into a capital T. Among the occasional grander variants are the churches at Lauder in Berwickshire with its Greek cross plan and central tower (1673), and Gifford, Lothian (1710), where the tower stands against the top of the T, behind the pulpit; both were paid for by noble landowners. Often a family aisle added to an old church has survived when the rest has been rebuilt, and the same may apply to valuable dressed stone features like belfries which are sometimes re-erected on the gables of later kirks. While not very many of these churches are of more than local importance, admirable in their siting and their relation to the houses of whose common materials they are built, the national importance of the *sum* of them is overwhelming. Alness, Ross and Cromarty (1625, 1737, 1775, as the dates on a gable relate) is a lovely ruin, one of many recent casualties. But its empty rubble shell bears no relation save an archaeological one to the crisply harled building of fifteen years ago; it tells nothing of the trim interior with its scrubbed pews and tables, its panelled galleries and the small extravagance of the plaster fan on the ceiling.

62. Alness, Ross and Cromarty. Part of ceiling soffit over Novar Aisle, taken in 1966

64. Alness, Ross and Cromarty. 1625, 1737, 1775 are the dates carved on the skew of one of the gables. Photographed in 1966, just before the church was stripped and made into a tidy ruin

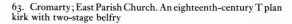

61. Cromarty; East Parish Church. Detail of pews and communion table

63. Cromarty; East Parish Church. An eighteenth-century T plan kirk with two-stage belfry

The parliamentary Union of 1707 confirmed the independence of the Church of Scotland. Among the outstanding churches of the eighteenth century are James Gibbs' St Nicholas West Church in his native Aberdeen (the nave of the old burgh kirk rebuilt, with a solemn arcaded interior, in 1755) and Allan Dreghorn's St Andrew's in Glasgow (1739). It is no secret that the latter, with its grandly integrated portico, its Glasgow version of a Gibbsian steeple and Clayton's lovely plasterwork, is in serious danger, for the *Church of Scotland Year Book* for 1976 shows that its congregation is linked with another and its communicants number a mere 221 – an alarmingly low figure.

But these are urban churches, of exceptional quality. The century's great achievement in church building was not the creation of many individual masterpieces but the continuance of the Scots tradition in a Georgian way. Churches are still related to other buildings by the prevalent use of harling, for example. But in towns and villages far and wide, especially those newly founded by

65. Fochabers, Morayshire. The Bellie Kirk by John Baxter, 1798, restored by Ian G. Lindsay in 1954 following the threat of demolition and the consequent public appeal

improving landowners, the Georgian church is the senior building by virtue of its formal position and varied geometry, and sometimes its spire or portico. These churches include William Adam senior's ingeniously cruciform church at Hamilton, Lanarkshire (1732); Gaelic and English churches back-to-back on the principal axis of the new town of Inveraray, Argyllshire with fastidious stone detail against the harling (Robert Mylne, *c.* 1794); the octagonal church at Kelso, Roxburghshire, the circular one at Bowmore on the island of Islay, and an infinite number of variations on the old T plan. Of many regional specialities, the box-of-bricks geometric spires of Ayrshire and the far south-west are one example. The eighteenth and early nineteenth centuries are the great period

66. Farr, Inverness-shire. 1774. Now a museum of the history of the Highland Clearances

67. Edinburgh; St George, Charlotte Square. Robert Reid 1811. Purchased by the Crown and converted for use as the West Register House, 1965

68. St Andrews, Fife; Holy Trinity. A mediaeval burgh church, elaborately recast for reformed worship in the eighteenth century

69. Plockton, Ross and Cromarty. A parliamentary church of about 1830 designed by Thomas Telford, listed in category A by the Secretary of State

of the Scots kirk, and the majority of small-town churches are in good heart. Yet the ever-present danger of a union, or rather of the consequent redundancy, is illustrated by the loss in 1956 of the square parish church by R. & J. Adam at Lasswade, Midlothian (1793) and the narrow escape of the Bellie Kirk which is the centrepiece of the Duke of Gordon's town of Fochabers, Morayshire (John Baxter, 1775, restored by Ian Lindsay). An even more vital test was the affair of St George's Church in Charlotte Square, Edinburgh, the monumental new-town church *par excellence* (Robert Reid, 1814). In the late 1950s dry-rot and virtual redundancy struck it simultaneously but the chain of responsibility held, and it led back to central government by whom the shell was repaired, converted, and re-opened as an extension to H.M. Register House in 1965 at a cost no greater than a new purpose-designed building. There is much to be said against dummy

buildings, but everything in favour of preserving this mighty townscape.

Episcopalian worship in the eighteenth century was a matter of loyalty. For those who were prepared to pray for King George, including English visitors of course, there were 'qualified chapels' like the one at Haddington, Lothian (1769). The earliest of these buildings is St Andrew's by the Green in Glasgow (1750), a pedimented church of great dignity with galleries and an eighteenth-century organ, blighted like its Scottish sister church by the decline of Georgian Glasgow, and finally by the plan for a section of the ring road which is unlikely to materialize. It was closed in 1972 and a plan for its future is now urgently needed. After 1792 Episcopal chapels were built in the larger towns and Edinburgh was particularly well furnished with them. The first was a pretty Gothick octagon by James Adam (1793), now a plumbers'

70. Bowmore, Argyll; Killarrow Parish Church. 1769. A circular church at the end of the main street

71. Glasgow; St Andrew's by the Green Episcopal Church. 1750. Now disused

72. Glasgow; St David's Ramshorn Church. T. Rickman, 1824. A focus of the Georgian townscape, its roll of communicants has fallen to a dangerously low level

warehouse, its congregation having united with that of Archibald Elliot's fine perpendicular church of St Paul (1818), further down York Place. But even the latter is now sparsely attended, St John's at the West End (William Burn, 1816) being the only flourishing member of this remarkable trio.

Stern measures were taken against Jacobites in 1716 and 1746, and the penal laws were not relaxed until 1792, four years after the death of Prince Charles; meantime they were defied, particularly in the north-east, by underground congregations. The Roman Catholics were granted freedom of worship in 1793, but their earliest buildings are less notable than those of the Episcopalians, belonging to the inter-denominational army of late Georgian Gothic churches whose great value is scenic rather than architectural. With their fire-screen fronts in town and their pinnacled towers in the country, they are familiar furniture whose worth has increased with time. James Gillespie Graham was one of their chief purveyors, but with the Lincolnshire Gothic tower and spire that he added to Montrose parish church in 1832 he showed that he was capable of something more; Montrose and St John's Tolbooth Church in Edinburgh (1841) are heralds of a serious Gothic revival in which one cannot escape the impression that Victorian Scotland is determined to make up her leeway in relation to mediaeval England.

Something must be said of the various independent movements, even before the great break of 1843. Pastor Glas built his original church in Dundee, Angus (1728) and John Wesley built Scotland's first Methodist church at Arbroath, Angus (1772). Both are octagonal. James Haldane built the first Congregational church in Edinburgh in 1799. Some sects were motivated, significantly as it turned out, by questions of relationship with secular

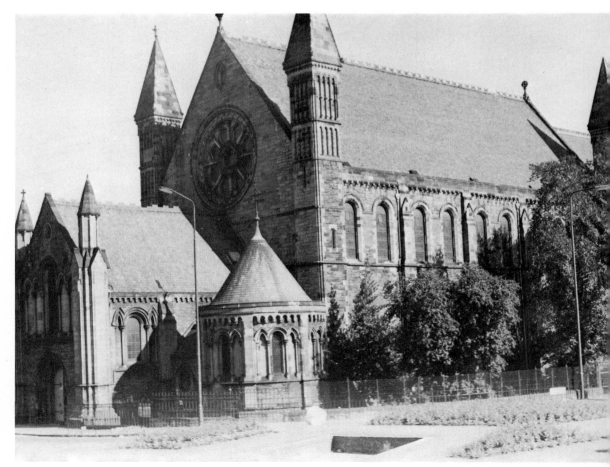

73. Edinburgh; Catholic Apostolic Church. Sir R. Rowand Anderson, 1875. Only the narthex and baptistery are now used by a Reformed Baptist congregation

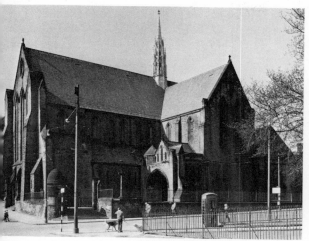

74. Glasgow; Barony Church. Sir J. J. Burnet & J. A. Campbell, 1886. Successor of the castellated church by R. & J. Adam

75. Glasgow; Barony Free Church. John Honeyman, 1866. Demolished 1967

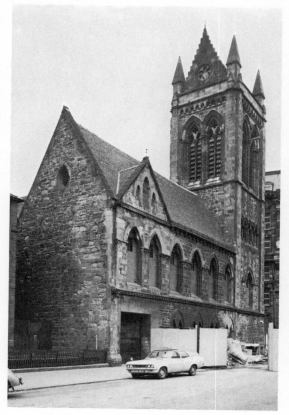

76. Glasgow; Former United Presbyterian Church, Caledonia Road. Alexander Thomson, 1856. Burnt out in 1965; a sad fragment preserved as a pious ornament by the local authority

77. Edinburgh; Barony and St James's Church. After losing its spire

78. Edinburgh; Barony and St James's Church. J. T. Rochead, 1859. It had already suffered some amputation before the crown spire was finally lopped off c. 1956, and is now a store for theatrical costumes

government. Thus the main body of Seceders was split in 1747 over the religious implications of the burgess oath; a fine, plain Burgher church (1806) survives after a fashion in Haddington, Lothian, as a British Legion club. At the turn of the century Burghers and Anti-Burghers broke up into the Old and New Lights. And meantime a division, in many ways a social one, had widened in the Church of Scotland itself.

At the Assembly of 1843 the Church split dramatically in two – a split that divided the great majority of congregations and created almost overnight the need for the doubling of church buildings in virtually every parish in Scotland. A rather austere Gothic was at first the hallmark of the buildings of the new Free Church, and it is seen at its most effective in Aberdeen where in 1844 Archibald Simpson designed the triple kirk which is the Free Church counterpart to the subdivided burgh kirk of St Nicholas. Its plain spire of dark red brick stands in the Den Burn valley amid granite classicism. Not one of its churches is still in use, and the present proposal is to retain the spire as a feature of a new (Gothic!) shopping centre. This is the most terrible example of the kind of architectural losses that continue to result from the 1929 Re-Union of the Church of Scotland and most of the Free Church.

The architectural achievements of the United Presbyterians, who were formed in 1847 and joined the Free Church in 1900, are among the most distinctive in Victorian Scotland. In Glasgow Alexander 'Greek' Thomson's St Vincent Street Church (1859) was restored at a cost of £80,000 and his Caledonia Road Church (1856) was consolidated as a partial ruin, both in the 1960s by what was then Glasgow Corporation. Of Frederick Pilkington's devout and astonishing Gothic churches the incomplete example at Penicuik, Lothian is probably the most extraordinary. Trinity Church in Irvine, Ayrshire (1862), rejected by the united congregation, was reprieved by voluntary, local and central government effort in 1975.

For the rest, Scotland's rich inheritance of Victorian and later churches can only be briefly mentioned. A great wave of Episcopalian enthusiasm, aided by much private

79. Isle of Cumbrae, Collegiate Church of the Holy Spirit. William Butterfield 1849. Maintained on an Episcopalian shoestring, the collegiate buildings assisted by a grant from the Historic Buildings Council for Scotland

80. Kirkintilloch, Dunbartonshire, 1644. Eighteenth-century woodwork. Now converted into a museum

81. Edinburgh; Holy Trinity, Dean Bridge. John Henderson, 1838. Used by the South of Scotland Electricity Board to house a transformer sub-station

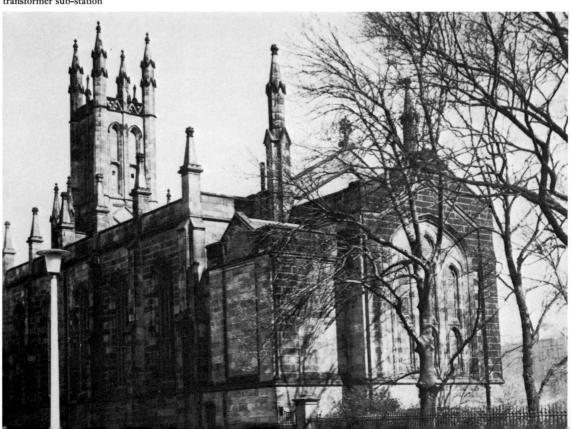

patronage, spread through Scotland and many of the well known giants worked there. Gilbert Scott, for example, took unaccustomed fire at two churches that later became cathedrals in Dundee (1852) and Glasgow (1871). Bodley was commissioned by Bishop Forbes at St Salvador's, Dundee, from 1857, and Butterfield by Lord Glasgow for the Collegiate Church of the Holy Spirit on the island of Cumbrae (1849). Bodley's principles were variously continued in the twentieth century by Lorimer, Harold Tarbolton and the Aberdonian architect Ninian Comper. Of Roman Catholic architects, Joseph Hansom made the most distinctive mark. Sir Rowand Anderson worked for both denominations and for what might be called the right wing of the Church of Scotland, as well as designing the prodigious Catholic Apostolic Church in Edinburgh (1874), now partially disused, its furnishings dispersed. And his scholarship was matched by many another Scottish architect so that Glasgow, for example, popularly known as a Victorian jungle but in reality a stronghold of creative academicism, is hardly less distinguished for Gothic than for classic churches. Only it must be confessed that to the Church of Scotland the later Gothic revival posed problems, for it found itself winning architectural prestige with churches that were far from suitable for reformed worship. There is a limit beyond which it is impossible to diversify the outside of a reformed church by means of aisles, galleries, staircases and vestries, and some over-complicated interiors were the result. Likewise the introduction of organs in 1866 was a mixed blessing, vast instruments often being moved in behind the communion table to dominate a whole church.

The value of Scottish churches is broadly acknowledged in the Secretary of State's Lists of Historic Buildings, which represent the nearest thing to a national inventory. Under the late Ian Lindsay as Chief Investigator, these included Victorian and later buildings from the start, though there are still some unbelievable gaps (e.g. St David's R.C. at Dalkeith, Lothian, by Hansom, 1853). As in England, however, listed building consent provisions do not apply to alteration or partial demolition of listed churches as long as they are ecclesiastical in use. Nor are grants from the Historic Buildings Council for Scotland generally available for churches in use, although the Council has helped Roslin Chapel (which is privately owned) and a number of secularized churches including Pilkington's at Irvine. Moreover a pilot scheme for aid to churches in use is now proceeding, albeit very slowly and on a tiny scale in relation to the whole problem. In two major cases, the Cathedrals of Glasgow and Dunblane, the Crown has stepped in to acquire and maintain a working

82. Leith, St Ninian. The steeple of 1675 now incorporated into a flour mill

church because the Ancient Monuments Board could not do so (a guardianship monument is by definition without a use).

Local authorities have not been quick to help churches under the 1962 Act (introduced to Scotland in 1967), but Strathclyde Region and Cunninghame District are now helping at Irvine, Edinburgh assisted the emergency repair of another of Pilkington's masterpieces at the Barclay Church, and Dundee gave handsomely to the internal restoration of St Salvador's; so did the Pilgrim Trust.

The problem of alternative use is especially difficult. A church whose architectural value is based on function is, for that very reason, hard to convert to other uses without loss of integrity. The Church of Scotland's practice in the matter of new use is quite definite. The General Trustees, to whom the ownership of all churches passed from the various heritors in 1925, have an overall responsibility for their upkeep while still used for worship; that is, for seeing that kirk sessions do this work properly. In general they do it well. But if a church building is no longer a church, i.e. if it is not justifying itself as an aid to worship, a union of congregations is encouraged. Their members' right to choose between two or more church buildings is very zealously guarded: 1,023 unions and 305 linkings have taken place since 1929. The building not favoured

83. Dundee, St Salvador's Episcopal Church. G. F. Bodley from 1857. The interior was consolidated and restored in 1972

84. Dundee; St Salvador's Episcopal Church. Detail of chancel roof

(probably whichever is the less convenient) becomes an asset to be disposed of for the benefit of the Church Extension Fund, to build new churches where they are needed (the best of these are excellent indeed).

Planning authorities, increasingly conscious of townscape and landscape, are in a key position. It is up to them, in a case where demolition or alteration for secular purposes is unlikely to receive their consent, to let this be known as soon as the possibility of union and redundancy is mooted. They should recognize and identify the great contribution made by church buildings to the town and country scene in their districts, and as far as possible enlist the help of everyone who benefits from a church building in seeing that it is not lost. The Churches for their part must forsake some part of their traditional independence and be open about their problems and their plans.

Alterations, about which a planning authority can do nothing except by persuasion, are another matter. Often, of course, these go under the name of restoration, and restorers have a great deal to answer for. Alteration for functional needs is only part of the story. The root of the trouble is in those simple concepts, too often shared and inspired by architects, of what is good (an old look, a new look, rubble walls, pastel shades, light oak, flood-lighting) and what is bad (pews, galleries, dark stain, Victorian glass, furnishings and lights, plaster, white paint).

Furnishing and decorating firms have some responsibility, and so do the paint manufacturers. Some of these have free colour consultancy services for decorative schemes – an excellent idea that has sometimes had unhappy results. St James's Church in Leith, Edinburgh (Gilbert Scott, 1868) is only one of the churches whose original, carefully designed colouring, with stencilled patterns to relieve the mass of the walls, has disappeared under a less effective and durable combination of sky blue and mustard. St Salvador's in Dundee, with its polychrome Bodley interior, would have been another had not the rector listened to the protests of the Scottish

85. Edinburgh; Barclay Church. F. T. Pilkington, 1862. A dramatic incident in the tenement skyline to the south of the city, its spire was restored after gale damage in 1974 with the help of Edinburgh Corporation

Georgian Society in 1972 and challenged them to produce a better answer. They did, and the congregation is well pleased. In no church or denomination, not even with the Roman Catholics, should this procedure be the exception. The trouble is that good advice is like gold, but far less easy to identify.

On the whole, the impecunious *laissez-faire* of the Episcopalians has done less harm to the integrity of church buildings than the highly democratic procedures of the more prosperous Church of Scotland (of the Roman Catholics I would not dare to speak, but I have yet to meet the priest who is not concerned about the building where he works). In theory at least, the Church of Scotland has the answer, though the sensible advice to congregations in the *Year Book* could well be expanded, being silent, for example, about any matters of existing architectural merit.

86. Inchinnan, Renfrewshire; New Church of All Hallows. Sir R. Rowand Anderson, 1899. A fine work of the most ecumenical of Scottish Victorian architects, demolished in 1964 to make way for the runway of Abbotsinch Airport

It does, however, urge congregations to consult the Advisory Committee on Artistic Questions on a number of matters. Like all voluntary committees, this one may have its defects and limitations. But surely it is on the right lines, even if its title does seem to confirm the general misconception that Art is something quite separate from practical matters. Given a further expansion of its historical awareness; given a small full-time staff, and an understanding with the architectural profession which in this subject must acknowledge their point of greatest weakness; and above all a good relationship with the congregation of every church, this is the rock on which to build, and an example to the other Churches.

WALES
by Elisabeth Beazley

The future of the buildings of the Anglican Church in Wales is the main concern of this chapter, but that of the Nonconformist Churches, which are such a vital part of the Welsh heritage, must not be forgotten. Nor should that of the Roman Catholic Church, whose position is similar to that in England and Scotland. The position of the Church in Wales is quite different from the Church of England and the future of its buildings is considerably bleaker, for three main reasons: historic, legal and geographic.

The Church in Wales is not part of the Church of England. Its disestablishment in 1919 was the culmination of a long struggle begun by Geraldus Cambrensis soon after the Celtic Church was Romanized and brought into the Province of Canterbury in the twelfth century. The assets, including church buildings, were transferred to the Representative Body of the Church in Wales to be held by it in trust for the bishops, clergy and laity.

With disestablishment went partial disendowment. All pre-1662 endowments, valued then at £3,455,000 were transferred to the county councils and to the University of Wales. The funds transferred to the county councils were called Church Act Funds, a title which can cause confusion since those outside Wales often imagine that they are exclusively for the use of the Church. They are not. Grants made from these funds usually go to support work connected with literature, the arts, history or social services. However, during the past ten years or so a more liberal interpretation of the Act of Disendowment has given direct benefit to the Church in several cases (St Mary's, Tal-y-llyn, in Anglesey, was one of the first to be restored with the help of a grant made by the county council from the Welsh Church Acts Fund).

Following disestablishment, the Church in Wales launched an appeal to replace the lost endowments. This raised £710,000; a big sum for a small country in the 1920s. A further appeal in 1953 raised another £650,000. But recent inflation has quite undermined the Church's financial situation. Coupled with this are the generally improved standards of living (in 1921 a wireless set was rare) and the necessity, in most rural parishes anyway, for the rector to own a car. The Church feels that it must put men before buildings, thus higher stipends are its first concern. At present a newly ordained priest receives a minimum stipend of £1,415 with a house and an allowance of £68 in respect of his expenses of office.

However, disestablishment has had financial implications more far-reaching in its effect on church buildings than can ever have been envisaged. Since the Church in Wales has no legal connection with that of England it is excluded from any benefits proceeding from the Pastoral Measure of the Church of England of 1968 and the Redundant Churches and other Religious Buildings Act of 1969. Therefore if an architecturally outstanding Welsh church be declared redundant it cannot be vested in the Redundant Churches Fund.

This Fund now has over a hundred churches in England vested in it; that is to say their care and maintenance are the Fund's responsibility. In all it has repaired or helped to repair 110 churches. Since it was established in 1969, expenditure has amounted to £1,200,000. What has been spent during that same period in Wales on the repair and maintenance of redundant churches? No-one knows. Nor does there seem to be much hope of any reserve being built up to form such a fund for repair and continuing maintenance, unless as in England, some central government funds become available. In England, one third of the proceeds of the sale of sites of redundant churches goes to the Redundant Churches Fund, subject to a ceiling in the first quinquennium of £100,000 and in the current quinquennium of £350,000. When a church in Wales is

87. Gresford; Denbighshire. A splendid parish church built by Lady Margaret Beaufort

88. Llangelynin, Caernarvonshire; the Old Church. Many parishes have two churches – a mediaeval building in remote country and a nineteenth-century church in a village

89. Gyffin, Caernarvonshire; St Mary. The celure or coved ceiling over the altar is a Welsh characteristic

90. Llangelynin, Caernarvonshire; the Old Church. Interiors often have a barn-like simplicity of great character

sold or demolished and its site is sold the proceeds may be spent on new buildings but not, apparently, on the maintenance of redundant churches as monuments. There are also some who feel this money should not be spent on buildings new or old, but only the on-going mission of the Church.

But the difficult financial situation is only one side of the coin. Consideration of the geographical distribution of the parish churches is all-important to the work of the Church. In those parts of Wales where the Celtic pattern of settlement prevails, many churches are very much less conveniently sited from the point of view of their parishioners than is usually the case in England. In Wales, the village focused on its parish church is rare; indeed, in the Celtic parts, most villages are nineteenth-century and it is a matter of chance whether or not they were built close to a church. The old pattern of settlement having been one of scattered farms and hamlets, the churches were often

remote from any dwelling. Instead they were built at the intersection of several field paths or mountain tracks, where they were accessible to several scattered settlements. Since the days of the motor car, many are now only accessible on foot. Other sites, which can never have been entirely practicable from the point of view of the congregation, mark the place where some seafaring saint began or ended a journey (St Patrick is responsible for several such), or beside some holy well or spring, perhaps revered long before the coming of Christianity. Others were originally the church of a Welsh *clas*, a Celtic monastery which may have been sited in some quiet place where the community could get on with its life without the interference of its traditionally quarrelsome relatives (the Welsh have never found unity to be a natural state of affairs). For these reasons, and there are many parallels in England, the buildings of the Anglican Church in Wales are often very inconveniently sited for modern use.

91, 92. Capel Newydd in the Lleyn Peninsula is the earliest surviving Nonconformist church in North Wales (1769). It was meticulously restored in 1956 and opened to the public

93. Llanfaglan, Caernarvonshire; St Baglan. The huge timbers of its porch make a nice contrast to its interior (fig. 105)

Conversely many Nonconformist churches and chapels stand proudly in nineteenth-century villages. They are often grand buildings with dramatic galleried interiors and raked floors designed thus so that the congregation could both see and hear. All pews focus on the pulpit. Some of these churches have great architectural merit. Nearly all have outstanding character, and this applies equally to their humbler counterparts built to serve remote communities in the depths of the country. Generally speaking, it is easier to be slightly more optimistic about their future. They are younger buildings, usually more conveniently placed, and planned with a caretaker's house alongside making day-to-day maintenance simpler. But they too are nearly always too large for their congregations – with their great galleries many chapels seat a thousand or more. Their huge advantage from the architectural point of view is that, if declared redundant, it is less difficult to find a new use for a Nonconformist church than for an Anglican.

This is partly because the conversion of what is usually basically a barn (as were the great Roman basilicas), with big Georgian-type windows, is far easier than that of a mediaeval building, and most Welsh churches are either mediaeval or Victorian Gothic.

Equally important is the fact that chapels are often separate from graveyards. The burial ground round a church is frequently not vested in the Representative Body. Under the Disused Burial Ground Act (1884) no building, other than an extension to a church, is allowed on land set apart for burials. It is also difficult (but not impossible) to get a burial ground deconsecrated so this may severely limit any other use for a church. An additional problem arises because most church sites were conveyed under the Places of Worship Sites Act of 1873. Twelve months after a church on such a site is closed, the site reverts to the estate out of which it was formed. Naturally enough it is not now always easy to determine

94. Capel-y-ffin, Breconshire. This tiny church is well cared for and supported by tourism

95. Llenengan, Caernarvonshire; St Einion. Has two good mediaeval screens

96. Capel Peniel, Tremadoc, *c.* 1808. One of the first buildings to be completed in W. A. Madock's model town

97. Llangelynin, Caernarvonshire; the Old Church. A Liturgical arrangement that survived the nineteenth century undisturbed

98. Llanrhychwyn, Caernarvonshire; St Rhychwyn. Redundancy threatens many small remote churches, whatever their condition

99. Wrexham Parish Church tower. A mediaeval tower to compare with any in England

100. Llantysilio; Valle Crucis Abbey. Ruins of a once grand church

the original owner. In the meantime, the Representative Body, as trustee, has to continue to insure the building in case anybody (whether or not he be a trespasser) should suffer damage or injury as a result of its being in a state of disrepair.

The wretched habit, now so prevalent, of claiming compensation in such circumstances has doomed many a ruin, secular and ecclesiastic. It is earnestly hoped that nervousness on the part of those responsible will not lead to the disappearance or destruction of more good ruins. This is a legal matter which should be soluble. Wales has one great advantage over England which she should seize upon. In England, once a church has been declared redundant, it is not allowed to remain standing (however good its structural condition) unless it is either vested in the fund or an alternative use has been found. But by contrast the phrase 'the church can be allowed to become a decent ruin' is spreading in Wales. Alas, this is too often a euphenism meaning that the church is to be destroyed but that the walls will be left standing to a height of three feet – a more unpoetic and architecturally annihilating result is hard to imagine. However, there are several splendid ruins in which services are held annually on the appropriate saint's day or during the summer holiday season. The Church of the Knights of the Hospital of St John of Jerusalem, a rose-covered ruin by the river at Slebech in Dyfed, is one such; Llandeilo Abercwmyn, Dyfed, south of St Clear's on the same pilgrim's route to St David's, another. Other churches, not yet ruined, come to life in the tourist season: Mwnt, also in Dyfed and near Cardigan, is utterly isolated for most of the year on a grassy cliff top; for a few summer weeks the grass becomes a huge car park for the bathing beach below. Then too the tiny parish church of Capel-y-ffin above Llanthony, Gwent, resounds to the clip-clop of hundreds of pony-trekkers as well as the buzz of cars. The island church of Llangwyfan in Anglesey has long been the object of a holiday scramble over the low-tide seaweed. The once utterly remote chapel of Soar-y-mynydd in the heart of one of the most desolate tracts of hill country in Britain is now on a scenic route from the new Llyn Brianne reservoir; hundreds, literally, sign its visitor's book each year. Indeed, tourism has given new appreciation of many previously little-known buildings.

The listing of churches protects those in Wales to the same extent as it does in England. In the view of the Welsh Office, once an ecclesiastical building included in the annexe to the statutory list as Grade A, B, or C ceases to be used for worship it cannot be demolished or substantially altered until listed building consent has been obtained from the local planning authority or the Secretary of State.

There is firm belief that the House of Lords Judgment on the Howard Church, Bedford (8 May 1975) would relate to churches and chapels of all denominations in Wales. The designation of conservation areas also gives some statutory protection to unlisted buildings.

About 800 churches in Wales have been listed since 1968. In the first listing these were chiefly mediaeval buildings with some seventeenth-century churches. The eighteenth century was a time when the Anglican Church was at low ebb. The nineteenth saw the beginning of the great chapel building era and, from the middle of the century, there was extensive church building activity too. In the new listings,* begun in 1975, many churches have been recommended for relisting and Victorian buildings have been included.

Listing is of value because it can delay precipitate action but legal protection cannot save a building unless there is an energetic wish on the part of the owner to do so. However, delay may prevent demise in a country where lovers of buildings are thin on the ground (the rural population as a whole is thinly scattered).

The fate of a church must involve more complex decisions that that of any other building – or indeed of any other man-made object. Who is to judge its practical use? In Wales there are remote parish churches of modest but genuine architectural value, in a good state of repair, and lovingly cherished by two or three parishioners, but whose closure may not be far distant. The argument is that those parishioners can drive or be driven to a church more conveniently sited from the point of view of others in the rural deanery, thus making it possible for the incumbent to make better use of his time: a logical attitude on several counts. But surely individuals do matter? And who can foresee the long-term needs of the church in the light of the future distribution of population?

There are other churches architecturally so splendid that their closure would seem unthinkable. But the members of neighbouring parishes are far too loyal to their own less distinguished buildings to think of abandoning them. Haverfordwest in Dyfed provides a fair example. St Mary's is one of the finest churches in west Wales. It has a congregation drawn from various parts of the town (which is not a big place), and is within a stone's throw of St Martin's and St Thomas's. Both have their own local

*Buildings provisionally recommended for listing since 1975 include: Grade A, St John the Baptist, Church Street, Cardiff; St Hilary's, Llandudno. Grade B, St Mary's, Chepstow; St Mary's, Bute Street, Cardiff; St Augustine's, Rumney, Cardiff; St Tudno's, Great Orme. Grade C, St Mary's, Whitchurch, Cardiff; St George's, and Holy Trinity, Llandudno.

101. Pembroke Terrace Presbyterian Chapel, Cardiff

102. Llanlestyn, Anglesey, Low relief of St Iestyn

103. Llandwrog, Caernarvonshire; St Twiog. Sumptuous Georgian monuments

congregations who would undoubtedly object most vigorously to centralization, on sound emotional grounds. They could also rightly claim that St Mary's, with its central site in the heart of Haverfordwest, suffers from traffic noise and is less convenient. But it is the sound spiritual and historic grounds (too often dismissed as 'emotional') which must be considered, along with the more mundane, if the Church as an institution is not to destroy itself along with its buildings. A congregation's wish for its services to continue, within its own building, is of a far more lasting duration than a priest's incumbency. Priests come and go; they retire at seventy. Congregations, however small, represent continuity of worship. There would be few Anglican buildings left in Wales if the present criteria had been used to judge their usefulness in the eighteenth century.

Incidentally, there is one small but very important voluntary body which has helped redundant churches in both England and Wales, namely the Friends of Friendless Churches. Some five Welsh churches have so far received substantial grants from this source. By providing the initiative for restoration the society has induced other bodies to subscribe (such as the Pilgrim Trust, County Councils, and the Representative Body itself). The Society assumed the responsibility for the repair of St Mary's Tal-y-llyn and Llantrisant Old Church in Anglesey and Llangua in Gwent; and has made a beginning with the rescue of Llandeilo Talybont in Dyfedor, West Glamorgan; it made a substantial contribution towards the repair of Manordeifi in Dyfed; and it has other Welsh churches in its programme for the future. The example of the Ministry of Works in saving Llangar (Clwyd) by taking it into guardianship (1967) should not be forgotten. However, some churches must inevitably go, though some people would challenge this assertion.

When a church is closed for public worship the cost of maintenance and insurance is borne by the parish – a burden which must make immediate disposal the only attractive answer. This continues until redundancy is declared. But first the Diocesan Churches Committee will have assessed the quality of the church with the advice of the Diocesan Advisory Committee, clarified the legal situation as far as is possible, and satisfied the bishop that their proposals for its future are acceptable. Since there is no money available, it would seem that these proposals can only be for the sale of the building, or for its demolition and the sale of the site. If the bishop then declares the church to be redundant (the consent of the Parochial Church Council having been given), the Diocesan Churches Committee will be responsible for maintenance

and insurance. Certainly it is in everyone's financial interest to sell (see below) or demolish as quickly as possible.

It is in the very careful assessment which has led to a declaration of redundancy that England has certain immeasurable advantages. First there is the financial benefit resulting from the contributions of the State and the Church and the proceeds of the sale of sites in the proportion 2:2:1, as administered by the Redundant Churches Fund. There is secondly the long experience of the members of both the Fund and of the Advisory Board for Redundant Churches, most of whom (including the chairmen of each body) are laymen. This second advantage which England has over Wales is an invaluable asset when dealing with problems which require both expert knowledge and judgement to an unusual degree. Here are two bodies, not immediately concerned with diocesan and parochial matters, who are deeply committed to the Church and its problems, giving their time free to judge which buildings should be vested in the Redundant Churches Fund and which should not. Such bodies, on a national level, which can stand apart but speak with the authority of experience do not yet exist in Wales.

A new use may then be the only future for a Welsh church. Despite the many difficulties already discussed some churches have been sold for other uses. They include:

St James's, Carnhedryn: small theatre and accommodation;
St John's Mission Room, Lampeter, Dyfed: residential purpose;
St David's, Llanddewi: dwelling;
St Thomas's, Briton Ferry, West Glamorgan: Chapel of Rest;
St David's, Miskin, South Glamorgan: telephone exchange.

Two churches have been sold and their sites cleared for redevelopment or environmental improvement. Site values in towns may make demolition an attractive financial proposition. Conversely a ruined town church, converted into a quiet garden, can be an oasis for city workers.

Sale or closure also brings the problem of the disposal of the contents of a church. Much is of singular beauty and interest: memorial tablets and grave slabs may well be best left if the building can become a ruin. Other objects are needed by other churches and would greatly enhance them, but they are not always in immediate demand. The diocese would then wish to store them for the future rather than dispose of them, probably to secular sources. But at present there is not even money available for their safe-keeping. A redundant church might itself provide such a

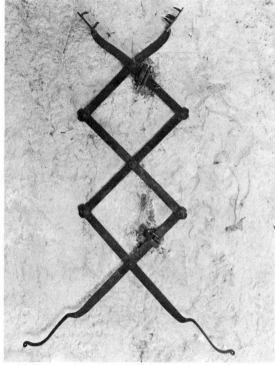

104. Clynnog, Caernarvonshire; St Beuno. Dog tongs

repository. It need not be heated but some simple form of dehumidifier would be necessary, particularly where joinery is to be stored. Early-nineteenth-century pews and other fittings have survived Victorian restorations in some Welsh churches, but their value is not always recognized. They are particularly vulnerable to rot. The few surviving oil lamps (admirably converted to electricity in a few churches) will be sought out by dealers if a watchful eye is not upon them.

'Improvements' to churchyards are referred to elsewhere in this book, but the anxiety for tidiness and easy maintenance has been behind what many would describe as vandalism in the graveyards surrounding some Welsh churches. Ironically, some have been cleared with grants supplied under 'Operation Eyesore'. Gravestones have been swept to the wall and 'landscaping' of the most banal kind substituted for the grey slate slabs which gave such a sense of continuity and belonging to the parish church. The fact that many churchyards are adorned with meadowsweet and cowparsley should be regarded as a bonus, not a disaster. Even nettles, a source of life for the peacock-butterfly and many other varieties, are a rarity to be cherished in some parts of Wales. In some regions the clearing of graveyards becomes an annual summer evening party towards the end of June. Llanfinangel-ar-arth is one such where a picnic supper in the churchyard follows the work – a fine mid-summer parish feast.

105. Llanfaglan, Caernarvonshire; St Baglan. Eighteenth-century pew ends in mediaeval church

106. Llanerchymedd, Welsh Presbyterian Church of Jerusalem. A typical galleried interior

Evening classes on the use of the bill-hook should go down as well in Cardiff, Aberystwyth or Bangor as in other towns where self-sufficiency inclined intellectuals live.

The problem of redundant churches is one to which the Welsh Assembly, if set up under devolution, might turn its attention, in conjunction with the Church in Wales and the Nonconformist Churches. The idea that a church building may be a vital part of the country's heritage, whether or not its use at the present time is practicable, needs as careful scrutiny in Wales as elsewhere. If the Turks, with the great legacy of Islam to maintain, can also care for some of the Christian churches which now lie within Turkey's national boundaries, surely we in Wales might take note. Any nation must cherish its heritage and when that heritage consists of buildings, the state must play its part. There are all sorts of ways in which this might be achieved in Wales. Once the maintenance of a redundant church is assured, there seems to be no reason why the Historic Buildings Council for Wales (given increased funds) should not extend its grant aid, now given only to secular buildings. County Councils may provide money from the Welsh Church Act Funds. There could be appeals to the Welsh nation (as against the individual denominations), and the Wales Tourist Board should surely contribute. This is a national problem and must be tackled as such. First we need widespread recognition of the fact that a church building may be of great value to the nation whether or not it is at present used for worship. (Doubters need only shut their eyes and imagine the Principality without a church or chapel in town or country.) From this recognition, and the will to cherish the best we have which must spring from it, sensible financial support will surely follow. Could not a small start be made now by selecting, say, ten of the best churches of any denomination which are no longer needed for pastoral work and assuring their future?

Comparison of the state of the Church in Wales now with that of 200 years ago must give rise to optimism in any rational mind. Then it was rent by spiritual crises leading to schism; many parishes were ignored by absentee clergy who often could not speak the language of their flock; buildings were closed or abandoned. When compared with the prospects of 1777, 1977 cannot but seem to be a bonanza for all Churches in Wales, except perhaps for those of us who cannot help but enjoy really bleak prospects.

MONUMENTS
by John Physick

'*Upon their Backs the ancient Statues lie,*
Devoutly fix'd, with Hands uplifted high,
Intreating Pray'rs of all the Passers-by.
At length they chang'd the Posture by degrees,
And plac'd the Marble Vot'ry on its Knees,
The Warriors rough devoutly Heav'n adore,
And Statesmen kneel, who never knelt before . . .
Next a less pious Posture they provide,
On Cushions lolling, stretch'd with careless Pride.
With wringing Hands the little Cherubs moan,
And Fun'ral Lamps appear to blaze in stone,
And Marble Urns with juster Beauty stand,
And rich Relievo shews the Master's Hand,
or the neat Altar with a Busto grac'd
In Roman Pride . . .' *J. Dart*, Westmonasterium, *1723.*

107. Great Brington, Northamptonshire; St Mary. Robert, Lord Spencer and his wife 1599, by Joseph Hollemans of Burton on Trent

Upon entering a church, one's first reaction, perhaps, is to flinch from the stare of the simpering androgynous angel in the stained glass window nearest to the door, but after absorbing the general atmosphere, the feel of the building, next to be noticed will be the monuments on the wall of the nave. It is these monuments, whether they be nineteenth-century white marble tablets, eighteenth-century mourning ladies, seventeenth-century gentlemen in wigs, sixteenth-century men and women of painted alabaster, or mediaeval knights and their wives, in stone, alabaster, or sometimes wood, or engraved in brass, or just carved stone coffin-lids, that more than anything else remind us of the hundreds or thousands of people who have worshipped in the building or its predecessor over many centuries, and who are buried in and around the building – the majority without any headstone or other memorial – and over whom we walk both in the church and the churchyard. In these days we hear so often that the church 'is for the living' (so much so that some incumbents now positively oppose the installation of any new memorial tablets), but always present in our minds must be those who, to the glory of God, built, maintained, beautified, or restored the buildings sometimes entirely at their own expense for future generations, and in whose debt we all now stand. But this is not all. As well as their historical, genealogical and sculptural interest, monuments afford splendid examples of the changing styles of heraldry, and of fashions in armour and dress.

The earliest monuments in most churches are usually to the feudal landowning families, such as the Fitzherberts at Norbury in Derbyshire, the Marneys at Layer Marney in Essex, or the Cobhams at Cobham in Kent, or occasionally to an ecclesiastic. But throughout the country are to be found the monuments and tombs of those who are a part of our history.

108. Ledsham, Cheshire; All Saints. Sir John and Lady Lewis, 1677 by Thomas Cartwright

At the beginning of 1869 the First Commissioner of Works asked the Society of Antiquaries to 'have the goodness to furnish him with a list of such Regal and other Historical Tombs or Monuments existing in Cathedrals, churches, and other public places and buildings, as in their opinion it would be desirable to place under the protection and supervision of the Government, with a view to their proper custody and preservation'. The Society had prepared such a list by 1872, limiting it to monuments of persons who died before 1760. Besides royal tombs the historical monuments were divided into nine classes – namely, all Archbishops of Canterbury and York, Lord High Chancellors and Lord Keepers, Lord High Treasurers, Chief Justices, Statesmen and Ambassadors, people eminent in Theology, Science, Literature and Art, Naval and Military men, eminent Merchants, and, finally, 'other persons of note'.

Many of the memorials to the royal family and men of note, are, of course, in cathedrals or Westminster Abbey, and do not concern us here, but a surprising number of even the earlier ones are in parish churches. In Sheriff Hutton, Yorkshire, for example, there is a small altar tomb with an alabaster effigy of Edward, Prince of Wales, son of Richard III, while in Aldworth, Berkshire, is the mutilated stone effigy of Sir Nicholas de la Beche, Seneschal of Gascony, Constable of the Tower of London and Governor of the Black Prince, who died in 1345.

109. Over Compton, Dorset; St Michael. Standing figure of Robert Goodden, d. 1828, who was patron of the living and a talented amateur architect

From the fifteenth century on we can note the increasing rise of new families who took over the high offices of state. Of the Lord Chancellors, Sir Thomas More's († 1535) monument is in Chelsea Old Church, Francis Bacon († 1626) is in St Michael's, St Albans; Heneage Finch, Earl of Nottingham († 1682) is at Ravenstone, Buckinghamshire; Lord High Treasurer James Ley, Earl of Marlborough's († 1629) altar tomb with effigies is at Westbury, Wiltshire; Sir Anthony Browne († 1548) one of Henry VIII's executors, is at Battle, Sussex; Sir Thomas Hoby († 1566), Ambassador to France, is commemorated in alabaster at Bisham, Berkshire; Sir Hugh Calveley († 1394), Admiral of England, has a tomb at Bunbury, Cheshire; while of London's rich merchants, Sir John Crosby († 1475) is in St Helen's, Bishopsgate, near Sir Thomas Gresham († 1579); Sir Paul Pindar († 1650) is remembered in St Botolph, Bishopsgate, and Sir Josiah Child († 1699) has a splendid monument by John Nost at Wanstead, Essex; the founder of Tonbridge School, Sir Andrew Judd († 1559) is another in St Helen's, Bishopsgate, and Chaucer's grand-daughter, Alice, who married William de la Pole, Duke of Suffolk, has a sumptuous monument at Ewelme, Oxfordshire.

110. Little Rollright, Oxfordshire; St Philip. Edward Dixon, d. 1647, and his two wives. Further east an early seventeenth-century canopied tomb-chest to another member of the same family

111. Ewelme, Oxfordshire; St Mary. Alice, Countess of Suffolk, d. 1475

From the Society of Antiquaries' list, it is interesting to find which counties contain the greatest number of VIPs. Bedfordshire has only two, Berkshire (with the unfair advantage of Windsor Castle) sixteen, but Essex with twenty and Surrey with twenty-six, neither with a cathedral, head the record in the south, with York in the north. The Essex list contains large sculptural monuments as well as simple ledger stones, or churchyard headstones:

Boxted, Sir Richard Blackmore († 1729), mural monument without an effigy.

Chigwell, Samuel Harsnett († 1631), Archbishop of York, an almost life-size brass.

Colchester, Holy Trinity, William Gilbert, MD († 1603) marble mural monument, not mentioned by Pevsner. This church is now a Community Centre.

Little Easton, Henry Bourchier, KG († 1350) 'cross-legged effigy on altar tomb'. Not identifiable from Pevsner.

Hatfield Broad Oak, Robert de Vere, Earl of Oxford († 1221) cross-legged effigy. Pevsner says this is 'very defaced'.

Ingatestone, Sir William Petre († 1572), Secretary of State, 'Fine marble altar tomb, with effigies of himself and wife in white marble'. Pevsner – 'very fine quality'.

High Laver, John Locke († 1704), 'churchyard, Marble gravestone enclosed with iron rails'. Pevsner says the 'tablet' is now in the church.

Leyton, Rev John Strype († 1737) ledgerstone, 'The Gravestone is hidden underneath the new floor of the chancel'.

Leigh, Sir Richard Haddock († 1714), Admiral and Commissioner of the Navy, a table monument in the churchyard.

Black Notley, John Ray († 1706), churchyard, stone tomb surmounted by an obelisk.

Romford, Sir Anthony Cook († 1576), monument with alabaster figures.

Roxwell, Sir John Bramston († 1654), Chief Justice, marble mural monument. Not mentioned by Pevsner.

Runwell, Sir Thomas Raymond († 1685) Justice of the King's Bench 'black stone slab, arms and inscription; The slab probably formed the top of an altar tomb'. Not mentioned by Pevsner.

Saffron Walden, Thomas, Lord Audley († 1544), Lord Chancellor, tomb of black touch stone.

Hempstead, William Harvey, MD († 1657), 'marble monument with bust' by Edward Marshall.

South Weald, Sir Anthony Browne († 1567), Chief Justice for Common Pleas, altar tomb under an arch between the chancel and north chapel, with effigy in brass of a lady – 'the figure of Sir Anthony gone. Perhaps moved from original position'. Not in Pevsner. Theydon Mount, Sir Thomas Smith († 1577), Secretary of State, effigy under canopy.

Wanstead, Sir Josiah Child († 1699), merchant, 'large and sumptuous marble monument with recumbent effigy; also a statue in a niche above' by John Nost.

Writtle, Sir John Comyns († 1740), Lord Chief Baron of the Exchequer, 'chancel, mural monument of marble with bust' by Sir Henry Cheere.

In all, the Society of Antiquaries listed 610 memorials of every type: the report of their Sepulchral Monuments Committee said:

'It will be seen that . . . we had regard not to the value of the monuments as were works of art, but to the importance of the persons commemorated as actors in the great drama of our national history.

'It was our belief that in any scheme for the protection of these monuments the object in view would be rather the conservation of the existing memorials of our more illustrious countrymen, than the mere gratification of artistic taste or antiquarian curiosity; and that in this respect the simple gravestone which marks the interment of John Locke was more worthy of record than any more sumptuous monument erected to a person who had left no trace behind him in the history of the country.'

As the list of monuments in this little-known report was not drawn up on an artistic basis, some memorials could well have disappeared during the hundred years since it was compiled. Moreover, a great number of the churches mentioned contain other important works: for example, only one monument was noted at Little Easton, Essex, but the church has several of interest ranging from a small brass to an early fifteenth-century priest, to seventeenth- and eighteenth-century pieces to the Maynard family, one with two life-size marble figures on either side of an urn, attributed to the sculptor Edward Pierce, and another of 1746 depicting Lord Maynard leaning on an urn, the work of Charles Stanley. Although only two monuments are recorded for Bedfordshire, there is nevertheless much of interest in the county, as at Flitton, where there is a famous series to the de Grey family.

During the last century any list of monuments compiled on an artistic basis would in all probability have been fairly exhaustive in mediaeval works, and might have contained a smattering of any later sculptures which had always been highly regarded, although these would have been re- latively few, especially the eighteenth-century ones which had by that time generally fallen from favour. In fact, until the 1920s, when Mrs Esdaile began her work in identifying sculptors of such monuments, they were too often dismissed as unworthy of attention. The Royal Commis- sion on Historical Monuments originally stopped short at 1714 when compiling its inventories, so that that of Westminster Abbey does no more than simply list (very briefly) what are the major memorials.

Regrettably, this attitude still persists. While rhapsodiz- ing about a decayed, stone, cross-legged knight, parish church guides tend to ignore anything from 1700 onwards. The current leaflet describing the charming parish church of Lullingstone, Kent, mentions the 'sumptuous tomb' of Sir John Peche, the 'great table-tomb' of Sir George Hart, and the 'heraldic memorial' of Percyvall Hart, but totally ignores the fourth work, an attractive and large wall monument in coloured marbles, with a relief portrait, of Anne Dyke († 1763), which is undoubtedly the work of Sir Henry Cheere, one of the foremost sculptors of eighteenth-century England. A few years ago, the writer called at a church in Worcestershire which has several important eighteenth-century monuments. At the door he met the incumbent and explained the reason for his visit, and was led straight to a small, early seventeenth-century mural alabaster. When pressed, the clergyman admitted that there were some others in what he described as the Chamber of Horrors, and expressed surprise that anyone would willingly look at them. It is hardly surprising, then, that monuments are sometimes not treated well. Not so long ago, the magnificent monument to Lord King († 1734) at Ockham, Surrey, by Michael Rysbrack, was surrounded by brooms and dustpans; at Stanmore, Middlesex, the immense four-poster tomb of John

Wolstenholme († 1663) was used as a convenient resting place for ladders, dirty tin vases and so on; and the strange memorial by John Stone in All Saints, Maidstone, in July 1976 had disappeared, no doubt temporarily, behind an enormous pile of organ pipes.

Since the Reformation when the provision of religious sculpture ceased, and much was destroyed, the history of British sculpture is largely to be found in sepulchral monuments. Although a work by almost every major sculptor can be found in Westminster Abbey, it is only by visiting the parish churches that one can see the whole sequence of British sculpture, properly and extensively. Several churches contain a surprising range, particularly when certain families are commemorated over a period of two or three hundred years, such as the family St John at Battersea in London, Bletsoe, Bedfordshire, and Lydiard Tregoze, Wiltshire; the Harcourts at Stanton Harcourt, Oxfordshire, the Brownlows at Belton and neighbouring churches in Lincolnshire, or the Russells, at Chenies, Bedfordshire. At Great Brington, in Northamptonshire, for instance, one can see monuments to the Spencers by Jasper Hollemans of Burton, Nicholas Stone, John Stone, Nollekens, Chantrey and Flaxman; at Warkworth, Northampton, the justifiably famous Roubiliacs; or at Harefield, Middlesex, where the memorials to the

112. Wetheral, Cumberland; Holy Trinity. Mrs Howard of Corby Castle, d. 1789, by Joseph Nollekens, in the private mausoleum of the family on the north side of the chancel

INTO THY HANDS I COMMEND MY SPIRIT: FOR THOU HAST REDEEMED ME, O LORD, THOU GOD OF TRUTH

MARIA,
THE 3ʳ DAUGHTER OF ANDREW, LORD ARCHER,
WAS MARRIED TO HENRY HOWARD, ON THE 22ᵈ OF NOVEMʳ 1788.
AND DIED WITH HER INFANT DAUGHTER,
ON THE 2ᵈ OF NOVEMBER 1789,
IN THE 23ᵈ YEAR OF HER AGE.
THIS TRIBUTE OF SORROW IS PAID
TO THE MEMORY OF HER WHO APPROACHED NEAR TO PERFECTION,
BY THE AFFLICTED HUSBAND AND SISTERS.

113. Throwley, Kent; St Michael and All Angels. Mary, Lady Sondes, d. 1603, possibly by a member of the Johnson family

114. Great Brington, Northamptonshire; St Mary. Sir Robert Cavendish-Spencer, d. 1833, by Sir Francis Chantrey

Newdigates were carved by William Stanton, Richard Hayward, John Bacon, Grinling Gibbons and Michael Rysbrack. at Harefield there is also a spectacularly lavish early-seventeenth-century catafalque to a Spencer daughter, Alice († 1636) (who married an Earl of Derby), dripping with heraldry, with the Countess, coroneted, on her bier, her daughters kneeling below, and all richly coloured. But it would be a great mistake simply to be interested only in those monuments whose sculptors are known. The greater number by far is as yet unattributed. No one has systematically begun to try to sort out the late-sixteenth- and early-seventeenth-century works by the Southwark school of sculptors such as the Johnson family, the Cures, Maximilian Colt and others. A few, too few, are certainly known to be the work of sculptors of this period, such as Gerard Johnson's tomb of the Fourth Earl of Rutland at Bottesford, Leicestershire, Epiphanius Evesham's monument to Lord Teynham at Lynsted, Kent, or that to the 1st Earl of Salisbury by Maximilian Colt, at Hatfield, Hertfordshire, but only because in these cases contracts, drawings or the occasional signature have survived. A very great deal of research has still to be undertaken, and it cannot be done if the monuments have disappeared and all we have left to look at are photographs. Is such a possibility too drastic? I do not think it is, for British sculpture is at risk through indifference, vandalism, dislike, the high cost of conservation, inflation, Value Added Tax, and the demolition of the churches which have housed it for so long.

Since the Reformation sculpture has always been vulnerable. First of all, there was the destruction of religious images. Monuments, mistakenly, were also attacked and, as is well known, Elizabeth I had to issue an order prohibiting further damage.

Archbishops, bishops, and others, were charged to enquire into what had been damaged, and if those responsible were still alive, to find out how 'able they be to repair and remedie the same'. The result was a period of stability, visibly presented in the great output of highly coloured Elizabethan and Jacobean monuments which were placed in our churches, although there was later a certain amount of vandalism during the Commonwealth – the Sondes monuments at Throwley, Kent, in common with many others, had their hands and feet lopped off – while there were, accidentally, considerable losses in the Great Fire of London.

The next period of danger to monuments came during the nineteenth century when the crumbling churches were enthusiastically restored. During this time many monuments were cut down in size, or removed to different

115. Great Brington, Northamptonshire; St Mary. Earl Spencer, d. 1783, by Joseph Nollekens, after G. B. Cipriani

116. Herstmonceux, East Sussex; All Saints. Weeping putto, on a base with attached colonettes

117. Belton, Lincolnshire; St Peter and St Paul. Sir William Brownlow, d. 1754, by Sir Henry Cheere

118. Sutton, Surrey; St Nicholas. Dorothy, Lady Brownlow, 1700, photograph taken before the monument was hidden behind the organ, c.1870

119. Therfield, Hertfordshire; St Mary. Splendid baroque monument, unusually in wood rather than stone or marble, to Ann Turner, d. 1677

seems liable to no molestation may, at the suggestion of an ambitious architect, an ignorant committee, or a speculator in glazed tiles, be turned inside-out – chantry chapels destroyed, and tombs needlessly removed, from the . . . graves which they once marked – the modest slabs which recorded the burials of persons . . . allowed to be broken and carried away, or even . . . the whole floor of a country church with all the inscribed flagstones may be permanently concealed by a new encaustic-tile pavement.' The Society gave as an example the marble slab at St Mary, Lambeth, 'the sole sepulchral monument of Archbishop Bancroft which was broken during the progress of works at the church in 1851, and no trace of it now remains'.

However, during this Victorian period of restoration, rebuilding, and enlargement not all was lost. It is true that several monuments were concealed behind organs, such as the large monument to Lady Brownlow († 1700) at Sutton, Surrey, which has not been visible for over a century, and the Purbeck marble knight, *c.* 1260, now beneath the organ at Toppesfield, Essex; one hopes that in the future, these will be revealed once again. But at Shipbourne, Kent, the huge marble monument to Lord Barnard, designed by James Gibbs and almost certainly carved by Rysbrack, was carefully preserved when Gibbs's church was demolished and rebuilt in 1880 for the Cazalet family. The monuments to naval men and dockyard officials dating from the seventeenth century which had been moved from the mediaeval church of St Mary's, Chatham, when another building was erected in the eighteenth century were just as carefully placed into Sir Arthur Blomfield's new St Mary's, at the end of the last century. Many other examples of such care for the memorials of the past could be quoted. Times have now changed for the worse and the future is uncertain.

The Second World War unfortunately damaged much, but losses continued afterwards – what happened to the monument to Sir Edward Russell († 1705), at St Dunstan's-in-the-East, London, which, having survived the destruction of the building, has now disappeared? Eastwell, Kent, was neglected during the war when the park was occupied by the army. In 1951 the roof fell in, and after eighteen years of apparent indifference to the fate of the important monuments (one of them undoubtedly the finest sculptural work of the early seventeenth century in Kent) they were offered a home in the Victoria & Albert Museum as a last resort, to prevent any further damage or loss. But at present, pressures are building up, and more than ever before they are in danger of vanishing for all time, in common with a considerable amount of other

positions and not always re-erected correctly. This happened, for example, at St Paul's, Clapham, but recently, on advice from the Victoria & Albert Museum, much has now been reassembled according to early evidence. The Society of Antiquaries was very alive to the dangers – 'Practically', their report stated, 'it is impossible to ascertain what particular monuments are especially exposed to danger from malicious injury, neglect, or misdirected zeal for "Church restoration". The custodians of these objects are constantly changing, and with a change of men comes a change of taste. A church which today church furnishings. Perhaps because they are often large and heavy monuments present special problems. When churches are declared redundant the monuments in them become, it is hoped, subjects of discussion and negotiation, although it is not at all clear to most people how strenuous and determined this is, or, indeed, if any decision is binding. upon the ecclesiastical authorities. Some churches, important as buildings, also contain important sculpture, and if taken over by the Redundant Churches Fund are thus safe and available to visitors, though a recent abortive visit to Croome d'Abitot, Worcestershire, where no-one knew who held the key, was a most irritating experience. Unfortunately this is becoming increasingly common as more and more churches are being kept locked against vandalism and theft, and all too frequently there is absolutely no indication of where the key may be found.

The problems come when the building is recommended for demolition. If it is of a mediaeval foundation it will probably contain a variety of monuments dating over several centuries. Understandably, incumbents of neighbouring churches do not want them – they are even probably secretly hoping to remove or shuffle around the monuments in their own churches during the present fashion for re-ordering exercises. Although its future is still uncertain Chatham parish church was declared redundant a few years ago, and has been recommended for demolition, except for its tower. So far as it is known at the moment, nothing has been settled concerning its monuments, which have been carefully preserved in the past during various rebuildings, as has already been mentioned. Perhaps these memorials, in company with many others throughout the country, have come to the end of their time.

In 1971, when opening an exhibition of Victorian church art at the Victoria & Albert Museum, the Dean of Gloucester, Chairman of the Council for the Care of Churches (now the Council for Places of Worship) said that he hoped that one day the Museum would have churches as branch museums, just as it has important houses (Apsley House, Osterley Park House and Ham House). So far, none has been acquired, but surely the Dean's suggestion must soon be considered seriously, although the financial implications are daunting. Then, important monuments which would otherwise be lost could be rehoused. It should also be a matter of policy that regional museums, or perhaps diocesan authorities, should acquire churches as area museums for monuments and other fittings through the Redundant Churches Fund and without paying out enormous sums of money. There are

120. Kensington, London, St Mary Abbots. The Earl of Warwick, d. 1721, by Giovanni Battista Guelfi. Moved from the old church after Sir Gilbert Scott's rebuilding

many churches now redundant, or about to be declared so, which, splendid as landmarks, or as examples of architecture, have no internal fittings of note, and could very well be used for such a purpose.

However, until such decisions are taken, much remains which can be done. In so many churches the monuments are dirty, damaged and neglected. Pieces which have fallen off them are not replaced, and in a very short time, these are lost, or taken away by a souvenir-hunting visitor. Not so long ago, the writer discovered that a heraldic beast on one of Nicholas Stone's finest monuments was loose, and being only small was light enough for only one person to be able to carry it off to his car, undetected – the church is isolated. Fortunately, the beast has now been firmly fixed back into position. In another church not far away, two cherubs were missing from the pediment of a late seventeenth-century monument. They were discovered discarded under a pew at the back of the church – they are now back in their original places. If this sort of thing is discovered, tell the incumbent and continue to make a fuss until something is done, for a little money spent at once can save a very great amount later on – write to the Parochial Church Council, the Diocesan Advisory Committee, the local paper, the archdeacon, or even to the bishop. It could well make all the difference between a complete work of art and one without fingers, or arms, or garlands, or heraldic shields, or even small effigies. The Council for Places of Worship (83 London Wall, London, E.C.1), will always be pleased to advise on problems of conservation, but it must be emphasized that nothing should be attempted, in cleaning, recolouring, or repairing a monument, without adequate advice, or expert assistance, and for most work a Faculty is essential – this will bring in the Diocesan Advisory Committee.

In conclusion, it will be remembered that the Society of Antiquaries was asked by the First Commissioner of Works for their list of monuments which might be cared for by the government. What was the result? By the time the report was submitted there had been a change of Commissioner, and the philistine Acton Smee Ayrton was holding the office. He had no high regard for architects, sculptors or painters, and was the First Commissioner who threatened Alfred Stevens with prosecution for taking so long to complete the Duke of Wellington's

monument in St Paul's Cathedral. Indeed, he seized the work and locked the sculptor out of his studio. It could not have come as a surprise, therefore, when the Society of Antiquaries was thanked for its report but told that it appeared 'that the communication addressed to you . . . by the direction of the late First Commissioner, was made without the authority of the Treasury having been at any time obtained, and that the First Commissioner has now been informed by their Lordships that they must decline to authorize him to undertake any duties in respect of the Regal and Historical Tombs or Monuments referred to . . . in the valuable Report. . . .

'However much it is to be regretted that the Society should have been induced to embark on such a laborious and important investigation without the sanction of the Treasury, the First Commissioner deems it right to add that their Lordships further observe, that the object contemplated could not, apparently, be accomplished without legislation, and that they have no intention either of introducing a Bill, or of laying before Parliament the Report which has been made by the Sepulchral Monuments Committee.'

So there the matter has rested for 104 years. The future of monuments in many of our churches is now so disturbing that urgent and serious action is required to safeguard them. Something that can be done very easily and swiftly is to check through the Society of Antiquaries' list and see what has disappeared, or has been mutilated (the Craggs monument in Westminster Abbey), or moved elsewhere (Sir Heneage Finch, Eastwell), and to extend the list from its terminal date of 1760. Other lists, on a county basis, should be drawn up on as catholic a brief as possible, for all monuments (whether by known artists or not, and of all periods) which absolutely must be preserved even if their sheltering church is demolished, converted, or re-ordered. So far little has been lost, but this is certainly not a reason for either complacency or inaction. To achieve the final aim may be more difficult, for unfortunately, there seems to prevail in certain circles an art-snobbish attitude to British sculpture – that it is not worth bothering about as, when compared to contemporary work in Italy, France, the Netherlands, or practically anywhere, it is poor in quality, inept, and unworthy of anything more than a passing regard.

121. Great Brington, Northamptonshire; St Mary. Sir Edward Spencer, d. 1655, by John Stone

METALWORK
by Claude Blair, Shirley Bury

The waves of destruction which have swept at intervals over English church metalwork, and plate in particular, were at their fiercest during the Reformation and its aftermath. Works in gold and silver, sometimes enamelled or bejewelled, which had been made by craftsmen dedicated to the service of the Church, were almost entirely lost to the cathedrals, abbeys, parish churches and other religious foundations. Much went when Henry VIII dissolved the monasteries, and more as a result of the extreme Protestantism shown in the religious policy of Edward VI's government, which was inclined to cap principle with expediency. The Privy Council decreed on 3 March 1550/51 (Old Style): 'forasmuch as the Kinges Majestie had need presently of a masse of money, therefore commissioners shulde be addressed into all shires of England to take into the Kinges handes such church plate as remaigneth, to be emploied unto his Highnes use'. A considerable quantity of mediaeval parish plate was either confiscated at this time or else converted into the first communion cups – regarded as being more appropriate to Protestant worship than chalices – though Edward's death in 1553 produced a respite. This unfortunately extended only through the short reign of Mary Tudor, and the accession of Elizabeth I in 1558 saw the beginning of a deliberate, and largely successful, campaign to compel all the clergy to convert their chalices into cups. The result of all these depredations is that this country retains not a single mediaeval treasury, nor a single shrine made of precious or semi-precious materials, of the kind that still survive on the continent, while fewer than 200 parish churches still possess pre-Reformation chalices or patens. Though it is clear that those churches able to retain their plate were obscure and not over-wealthy, owning in consequence nothing of the quality represented by the mid-thirteenth-century chalice and

paten found hidden near Dolgellau, Gwynedd, in 1890 and now in the National Museum of Wales, their holdings form a very considerable proportion of all the surviving pre-Reformation plate of any kind, and are of immense importance to the study of English silver. Many pieces are very handsome as, for example, the chalices for Hamstall Ridware, Staffordshire (c. 1360), Nettlecombe, Somerset (hallmarked 1479, the earliest recorded London date-letter), Coombe Keynes, Dorset (c. 1500) and Leominster, Herefordshire (c. 1510).

The effects of the Reformation and the further depredations of the seventeenth-century Puritans, though devastating enough, were not quite so comprehensively destructive of other types of church metalwork. Excluding small excavated pieces, probably more than 90 per cent of the base metal objects surviving from before the Reformation in Britain are in cathedrals and parish churches. If they had not been preserved there we should know virtually nothing of the actual products – as opposed to descriptions in documents – of mediaeval founders, latoners, plumbers, blacksmiths and armourers in this country, and together they form a unique corpus of material that is still a long way from being completely studied, or even fully recorded. Not all the objects concerned were, in fact, made in this country, but even those that can be shown to have been made abroad are of great importance for the information they provide about foreign influences on the products of native craftsmen.

The comparative survival rate of different groups of objects has been quite erratic. There appears to be no pewter, and brass chandeliers and candlesticks are excessively rare, though the reason for this has probably as much to do with lighting improvements as with iconoclasm: on the other hand, brass lecterns, brass and bronze door-closing rings, bells and lead fonts, survive in

123. Patshull, Staffordshire; St Mary. Silver flagon by Paul de Lamerie, 1724–5

surprisingly large quantities. Most are of high quality, and a few are masterpieces: for example, the closing rings at Dormington, Herefordshire, and formerly in St Nicholas Church, Gloucester (now Gloucester Museum), which date respectively from the twelfth and early fourteenth centuries, and the Romanesque fonts at Dorchester, Oxfordshire, and Tidenham, Frampton and Sandhurst, Gloucestershire. The existence of these gives some indication of the technical and artistic traditions that lie behind the more famous masterpieces of the English mediaeval founder's art such as the Gloucester candlestick in the Victoria & Albert Museum and the great gilt-bronze effigies in Westminster Abbey and St Mary's, Warwick.

The practice of suspending a gentleman's crested helmet, gauntlet, shield, coat-armour, spurs and sword over his tomb as a memorial (*achievement*) is responsible for the survival of all the existing mediaeval armour, apart from a tiny handful of pieces, known to have early associations with this country. The most famous examples are the helms of the Black Prince, in Canterbury Cathedral, and Henry V, in Westminster Abbey, but many parish churches also possess important late mediaeval and early-sixteenth-century headpieces. (The majority are associated with late-sixteenth- and early seventeenth-century tombs. The reason is that by this period the heralds, who organized the funerals, normally provided the achievement and were in the habit of buying up obsolete armour for this purpose.) However, a recent spate of thefts of church armour is leading to more and more of them being deposited in museums. None can be shown to be certainly English, but it is extremely likely that many were made here, including probably the two late fourteenth- or early fifteenth-century helms at Cobham, Kent. There can be no doubt, on the other hand, that some were imported from northern Italy or Flanders, among them the sallet skull at Eardisley, Herefordshire, which bears an Italian mark, the sallets at Blithfield, Staffordshire, and Witton-le-Wear, Co. Durham, and a magnificent series of late-fifteenth- and early-sixteenth-century tournament helms, of which there are examples at Ashford and Cobham, Kent, Melbury Sampford, Dorset, and Broadwater, Sussex (recently acquired by the Tower of London Armouries). It should be noted that, until recently, the helms were regarded as being English in origin because the majority of recorded examples are preserved in English churches.

Mediaeval English decorative wrought ironwork, like mediaeval English armour, barely exists outside churches. Of all types of metalwork it is probably the least appreciated and no fundamental new study of it has been

124. Gloucester; St Nicholas. Early fourteenth-century bronze closing ring, now in the City Museum

125. Dorchester, Oxfordshire; St Peter and St Paul. Twelfth-century lead font

126. Dormington, Herefordshire; St Peter. Bronze closing ring, twelfth century

127. Broadwater, Sussex; St Mary. Late fifteenth-century Flemish tournament helm from the tomb of the eighth Lord de la Warr (d. 1526)

128. Elford, Staffordshire; St Peter. Victorian altar rails. Both Salvin (1848–9) and Street (1869–70) carried out work on the church in the 19th century

made since the pioneering work of J. Starkie Gardner was published at the end of last century, though a number of general books based on his work have appeared. This lack of interest is difficult to understand, for much of the ironwork is of considerable artistic merit, with a strong feeling for linear design. Notable examples are the remarkable eleventh- or twelfth-century doors at Stilling-fleet, Yorkshire, and Staplehurst, Kent, the twelfth-century geometric designs at Little Hormead, Essex, and Skipwith, Yorkshire, and the superb foliated scrollwork – probably made by the late-thirteenth-century royal smith, Thomas de Leighton – at Leighton Buzzard and Eaton Bray, Bedfordshire.

Several thousand mediaeval monumental brasses still remain in English churches, far more than in the whole of the rest of Europe put together. Their survival is all the more remarkable since the destructive zeal of the Puritans was succeeded by an equally damaging interest displayed by certain collectors and antiquaries. The *Torrington Diaries* (IV, p. 41) contains the following passage describing one thwarted attempt at acquisition: 'Return-ing to Cople Church We stopp'd for the inspection, in which are . . . some brasses – but *none* that would travel.' Nor were the clergy always helpful about preserving their treasures, as is demonstrated by an incident recorded in the *Transactions of the Monumental Brass Society* in September 1890, in which the incumbent of Godmersham Church dealt with a suggestion made by an official of the Society that a loose inscription be fixed by recommending him to 'amalgamate the Society with another called the "Anti-poking the Nose into other people's business Society"'.

The mediaeval brasses are probably the most studied of all kinds of early metalwork because of the present widespread enthusiasm for brass-rubbing – an enthusiasm which, incidentally, is beginning to cause conservation problems – and certainly the only ones to have their own learned journal. Despite this, art historians in this country

129. Leighton Buzzard, Bedfordshire; All Saints. Thirteenth-century iron door mounts by Thomas de Leghtone

have always been inclined to treat brasses with a certain amount of disdain as mere sources for the study of costume, armour, heraldry and genealogy, rather than works of art in their own right. This attitude is as insensitive as the fustian antiquarianism of past generations of brass specialists which was partly responsible for it, and there are welcome signs that it is less prevalent than it used to be. It has yet, however, to be fully appreciated that brasses are as much a part of the history of engraving, if a somewhat specialized one, as are prints, and that many of them are, in fact, masterpieces of the engraver's art. Notable examples, among many, are the military brasses at Acton, Suffolk, Stoke D'Abernon, Surrey, and Chartham, Kent – all now dated to the second and third decades of the fourteenth century – and the ecclesiastics at Higham Ferrers, Northamptonshire (1337) and Cowfold, Sussex (1433).

It will be clear from the foregoing that the role of the parish churches as preservers of pre-Reformation de-

corative metalwork in this country has been absolutely crucial. Where the preservation of later metalwork is concerned, their role has still been important, for they have acted as custodians of some superb examples of most of the major crafts: pewter, clocks, brass chandeliers and lecterns, ironwork and plate. Designed mainly for ecclesiastical use, in terms of the national inheritance these furnishings complement the treasures that have remained in the possession of various secular institutions and long-established families. In addition the Church has harboured crafts for which there is no real secular equivalent. One such is that of the brass-engraver which, after a serious decline in the first half of the sixteenth century, was revived during the reign of Elizabeth under the influence of immigrant craftsmen such as the Johnsons of Southwark. The craft died out in the seventeenth century but was resuscitated once again by the mediaevalists of the Victorian age. Another instance is the craft of the armourer: apart from the special case of the armour made in the Royal Armouries at Greenwich, the greater part of the extant sixteenth-century armour with identifiable associations in this country is represented by helmets and gauntlets hanging over tombs in churches.

Nevertheless, the case of the unhelpful vicar who objected to advice being offered about his brass is not an isolated example. The churches' custody of their treasures since the Reformation seems sometimes to have been arbitrary. But there can be no doubt of their importance as patrons. Goldsmiths in both London and the provinces did extremely well out of the conversion of the old Mass plate into communion cups of the required Protestant form during the reigns of Edward VI and Elizabeth I. Some indication of the scale of the exercise is shown by the fact that some 2000 of these cups made before 1578 have managed to survive up to the present day. The shape of the cups, modelled on secular types, created a paradigm from which there was little general departure for more than a hundred years, with the exception of the work produced under the influence of Bishop Lancelot Andrewes in the seventeenth century, which will be discussed presently. In the eighteenth century church plate remained conservative – the asymmetrical shapes of mid-eighteenth-century rococo designs were largely ignored, even in the later work of Paul de Lamerie, one of the most advanced exponents of the style in domestic silver (a chalice and paten made from de Lamerie's design for Sir Benjamin West in 1747 is in Melbury Osmund church, Dorset). What changes there were, were the outcome of doctrinal and liturgical developments. The use of household bread in the communion service, authorized by the second

130. Staunton Harold, Leicestershire. Mid-seventeenth century London plate: chalice and paten, plate and cover, alms dish, flagon and a pair of candlesticks

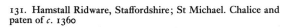

131. Hamstall Ridware, Staffordshire; St Michael. Chalice and paten of *c.* 1360

132. City of London; St Mary Aldermary. Communion cup and paten lid, silver-gilt and enamel, 1549–50

Prayer Book in 1552, led to larger patens than had obtained in the Middle Ages, and, as with the cup, they were modelled on secular examples. As the administration of the sacrament to the laity often meant that the cup had to be replenished with wine, flagons were of necessity much bigger than the mediaeval mass cruets which had served the priesthood alone. Many churches were unable to afford such a large vessel in silver, a circumstance recognized, for instance, in Archbishop Whitgift's articles for the deanery of Shoreham, West Sussex issued in 1597, which enquire after 'two comely pots of silver or pewter to fetch wine to serve the Lord's table, reserved and kept clean to that use only, being no tavern pots'. Comparatively few churches could afford to commission even one silver flagon and many parishes never managed to acquire anything more precious than a pewter flagon or later, towards the end of the eighteenth century, a vessel made of Sheffield plate (copper with a fused plating of silver). Benefactors sometimes came to the rescue, offering secular vessels such as the handsome pair of livery pots hallmarked in 1594 and 1597 which were given in 1630 to Westwell Church, Kent by George Baker, who lived in the parish. The fact that these flagons were secular in origin was used as an excuse for selling them in 1968. Happily they were acquired by the Goldsmiths' Company, but the flow of outstanding works on the market in recent years has put great strain on the financial resources of museums and other institutions concerned to preserve such treasures for the nation. This is a subject to which we shall revert later, only citing here a more recent instance, the sale of plate in 1976 by the church of St Benet Fink, Tottenham. The plate, originally the property of the City church with the same dedication which was demolished in the nineteenth century, passed into the possession of the Tottenham church when it was built in 1912. Among the pieces were two silver-gilt flagons of 1658 bearing the inscription: 'George Holman Esqre gave £100 to the parish of St Benet Fink for the ornaments of ye church whereof the flagons are part for the use of the communicants'; the sale was allowed on the grounds that the tie had been severed with the demolition of the church and that, moreover, the plate had not been used at a service in the memory of the present parishioners. The London Museum hoped to buy the flagons, but it could not afford to when they were auctioned with the chalices and patens of the remainder of the plate.

Turning to other silver furnishings, it must be said that altar dishes and candlesticks were rare outside cathedrals and collegiate foundations, but alms basins, knives and strainer spoons were owned by the more prosperous

133. Acton, Suffolk; All Saints. Brass of Sir Robert de Bures, second or third decade of the fourteenth century

134. Cirencester, Gloucestershire; St John the Baptist. Chalice and paten by A. W. N. Pugin, Birmingham mid-nineteenth century

churches. Despite the difference between the holdings of rich and poor parishes it appears from Charles Oman's *English Church Plate 597–1830* (1957) that by the beginning of the nineteenth century the Church had largely made good the immense losses incurred almost three centuries earlier. Some of the replacement plate was once again destined to be reduced and re-fashioned in accordance with new ideas, for an appreciation of historic silverwork was by no means widespread in the early Victorian era.

The change came after 1840, when for the second time in the history of the Anglican Church the ceremonial and ritual practised before the Reformation was the subject of serious attention by theologians. In the seventeenth century the interest in the early Church shown by Lancelot Andrewes, who held three bishoprics during the reign of James I, was reflected in some splendid services of communion plate made in his lifetime and afterwards. One of the most impressive of these services was commissioned in 1640 and 1654 by members of a Royalist family, the Shirleys, for the chapel they built at Staunton Harold, Leicestershire. The nineteenth-century Oxford or Tractarian Movement, which developed a predilection for

furnishings banned since the Reformation, was severely shaken by the secession to Rome in 1845 of one of its leaders, John Newman. Doctrinal considerations apart, the Oxford Movement might have done little more than set up a short-lived fashion for Gothic design in a Church still dominated by clergy with evangelic leanings, but for the activities of a group of men with Tractarian sympathies who formed the Cambridge Camden Society (later the Ecclesiological Society) in 1839. Deliberately refusing to engage in doctrinal controversy, the Society pursued what was known as the science of ecclesiology, that is, of church furnishing, but it was of such a type as to raise howls of rage, coupled with accusations of Popish practices, from convinced evangelicals. To an extent its critics were justified, for the Society was unofficially helped in its early days by the architect and designer A. W. N. Pugin, who had been converted to Roman Catholicism in 1835. Purgin was steeped in mediaevalism, and it was his mission in life to laud Gothic as the only fit style for a Christian country. His first clients were members of the Catholic community, freed from the civil disabilities under which they had lived by the passing of the Catholic Emancipation Act of 1829. The institution of the hierarchy followed in 1850, but the traditional fear of Popery among Anglicans was not easily dissipated, and Pugin's first Tractarian patrons went to extreme lengths to avoid their patronage being generally made known. E. E. Estcourt, a young Oxford graduate who went as a curate to St John Baptist, Cirencester, Gloucestershire early in 1842, wrote three years later to Pugin's manufacturer, John Hardman of Birmingham, to enquire about 'a chalice, chaste and good, to cost about £18 or £20 . . . of a good ancient ecclesiastical form . . .'. When the chalice was ready for delivery some two months later Estcourt asked Hardman's to 'be so good as to prevent any card or paper being placed in the packing-case which may lead to the discovery of its coming from your well-known manufactory – or even from Birmingham'. Estcourt himself became a Roman Catholic, but the chalice remains in the church for which it was commissioned.

The activities of Pugin and of the Anglican ecclesiologists were so remarkably successful, despite powerful opposition, that even their fellow antiquaries occasionally professed resentment at the spread of Victorian medi-

aevalism, one of them remarking to a colleague in 1847 that 'between us I am heartily sick of Gothic . . . it is all humbug every bit of it', but the Gothic revival swept on, and by the end of the century it was an unusual church that did not possess at least a chalice and flagon in the mediaeval manner, sometimes richly ornamented with enamels or set with stones taken from jewellery donated by pious ladies of the parish. The best examples were designed by Pugin and other leading architects such as William Butterfield (plate at All Saints, Margaret Street), William Burges (St Michael, Brighton) and G. E. Street (Colton Church, Staffordshire). The brass and ironwork by these and other designers of the period is equally striking. The high quality of much nineteenth-century plate and base metalwork has been recognized too little and too late to prevent unnecessary losses. It was inevitable that some old plate and furnishings were sacrificed to the Gothic interest, for Pugin's view that anything in the classic style could immediately be dismissed as 'pagan' struck a responsive chord in the movement. A chalice designed by Butterfield and shown at the Great Exhibition of 1851 was

135. Tarrant Hinton, Dorset; St Mary. Lectern in convinced Art Nouveau style, given in 1909

136. Sedlescombe, East Sussex; St John the Baptist. Local cast iron ledger slab to seventeenth-century members of the Bishop family

purchased by the parish church of Boston, Lincolnshire, with the proceeds from the sale of a 'silver-gilt bowl' dated 1776 (it was probably an alms dish). In Gloucestershire the church of St Denys, Little Compton, acquired in 1863 a chalice, paten and flagon in the Gothic style made partly out of an old chalice and a silver dinner plate without the legal sanction of the diocese. Several other examples are equally well documented. That more Anglican plate was not reduced was due to two main factors. Firstly, much Gothic zeal was expended on building and furnishing new churches in towns which had grown up in consequence of the Industrial Revolution, though it must be confessed that this onerous task went hand-in-hand with a passion for restoring old churches. Secondly, existing churches not rich enough to afford a new set of communion plate to add to their old could often rely, as in the past, on the generosity of a rich parishioner. Thus old plate was usually saved because there was no need to melt it down.

Towards the end of the century, when the mediaevalists were succeeded by the designers and silversmiths of the Arts and Crafts Movement, the historic value of plate was well recognized, and there is no record of their agreeing to make articles out of old church silverwork. The work of C. R. Ashbee and his Guild of Handicraft (chalice at St James, Chipping Campden, Gloucestershire), Henry Wilson (chalice at St Bartholomew, Brighton) and others testifies to the continued interest of the Church in modern design. The tradition has been continued, more recently by living silversmiths such as Leslie Durbin (plate at Askham Bryan Church, Yorkshire) and Robert Welch (plate at St Mary's, Swansea).

While plate was, on the whole, spared from the crusading enthusiasm of the Mediaeval Movement in the nineteenth century, the same cannot be said of all other metal furnishings. Ironwork was never as widespread as plate in churches, but by no means all that was made has survived. To cite only one example, tomb railings dating from the sixteenth and seventeenth centuries often disappeared in the rage for restoration; but among the work that was spared are a number of fine civic sword-rests as well as screens and sets of railings, and at least one superb font-cover (by Robert Bakewell, in St Werburgh's Church, Derby) to represent the work of some of the most eminent blacksmiths of the seventeen and eighteenth centuries. The fine brass chandeliers which by 1830 adorned about 1000 churches in England and Wales were subsequently reduced to some 300, largely because of the introduction of gas lighting. Some were re-hung elsewhere: one given to St George's Chapel, Great Yarmouth, in 1741 was removed when the building was restored in 1882 and

137. Derby; St Werburgh. Early eighteenth-century wrought iron font cover by Robert Bakewell

acquired by a clergyman who gave it to Hevingham Church, Norfolk, where it remains. Among other types of metalwork, pewter and turret-clocks have been until quite recently the least appreciated and the extent to which pieces of major importance have suffered from neglect, destruction and loss is uncertain.

Criticism of nineteenth-century practice is unwarranted when our age is currently witnessing the disposal of church treasures on a scale unparalleled for centuries. Unlike the reformers of the sixteenth or the Puritans of the seventeenth century, we can lay no claim to divine guidance; nor can we convincingly justify the rate of loss on the grounds of the new liturgical arrangements, or even of technology. Both the Anglican and the Nonconformist Churches, suffering from declining congregations and rising expenses, have necessarily had to close churches and disperse their contents. What is less acceptable to many is the way in which the major plate remaining in churches not so far threatened by redundancy is treated, not as an inheritance on trust, but as a saleable legacy, regardless of the original intention of the donors and of the sacramental function it has performed in the past. The exploitation of plate for church building, repair and furnishing coincided with the realization of its antique importance, so that while Ashbee and his contemporaries were emphasizing its value on aesthetic grounds, some parishes were already taking a more worldly view of the matter. In the porch of West

Malling Church, Kent, is fixed a stone tablet depicting an Elizabethan pot and the following inscription, dated 1903: 'THANKS·BE·TO·GOD·THE·PORCH·AND·PEWS·OF·THIS·CHURCH· WERE·MADE·BY·THE·SALE·OF·A·JUG·HAVING·SILVER·MOUNTING· WITH·THE·LONDON·HALL·MARK·FOR·1581'. To judge from an engraving of the piece which was published in *Archeologica Cantiana* in 1886, the jug, which was given to the church some time in the seventeenth century, was an exceptionally handsome piece, and by present standards of value the churchwardens made a poor bargain. But the jug was one of the first pieces of secular origin to be sold to raise money for the fabric of the church, a practice which has steadily grown in recent years. A *tazza* of 1551 from Deane, Hampshire, sold in 1970, is now in the Cecil Higgins Museum, Bedford, and the unique gold acorn-cup of about 1610 from Stapleford, Leicestershire, which came on to the market in 1957, is now in the British Museum. But acquisition has naturally depended on the purchasing institutions being able to raise the necessary funds at the right time, and as prices rise this becomes correspondingly difficult, if not impossible. The sale in July 1976 of a silver-gilt tankard of 1602 which was given in 1830 to St Andrew, Heddington, Wiltshire, set a new standard of prices which can only cause distress to everyone desirous of seeing that such pieces pass into public collections in default of their remaining in Church ownership. It is hard to reconcile the decision to sell with the inscription on the tankard which records the express intentions of the donor, the Rev. James Rogers, 'who with his ancestors for many generations have been Patrons and Rectors of this Church', and who dedicated the piece 'with pious reverence to the service of the Altar, for ever.' But it was sold for £21,000, more than twice the estimate.

Valuable plate is admittedly expensive to guard and to insure, yet there are several ways in which parishes can retain ownership of their silverwork at little or no expense to themselves. Since the last war, the Goldsmiths' Company has made generous grants towards the establishment of cathedral treasuries, thus giving churches in their dioceses the opportunity of lending their finest pieces for display. Museums throughout the country are usually happy to borrow plate and to make it available to the churches concerned for special festivals. So far, however, the erosion of our cultural heritage continues. In 1974, concerned at the losses of both ecclesiastical and secular plate from the Anglican Church, the Council for Places of Worship appointed a working party to consider the question. Its final report, which recommended a number of safeguards designed to bring home to parishes the full significance of their proposed sales, was formally adopted

138. Cheldon, North Devon; St Mary. Fine ironwork in remote church

by the General Synod. For a while its recommendations were effective, but revisions are necessary.

The facilities for loans to museums have recently been taken up by Nonconformist churches, and it is to be hoped that an increasing number of Roman Catholic churches will find it possible to deposit their treasures in the same way. With good will and a measure of persistence we may be able to rescue some part of our reputation with our successors. Otherwise we shall be fortunate if our age does not qualify as one of the most notable periods of iconoclasm.

WOODWORK
by Simon Jervis

Wood is an organic material, vulnerable to heat, frost, damp and insects. And what survives the dangers of warping, twisting, rot and infestation is an obvious target for burning or smashing by iconoclasts, vandals and restorers. Moreover, in a church, a building intended as an earthly expression of the eternal, wood must always seem an ephemeral substitute for the permanence of stone.

Thus of all the timber churches which dotted England before the Conquest but one solitary relict remains, St Andrew, Greensted, in Essex, built of split oak logs set vertically in an oak sill. Later examples are far from common. St Oswald, Lower Peover, and St James & St Paul, Marton, both in Cheshire, are the earliest surviving timber-framed churches, both dating from the fourteenth century: timber-framing also survives in a few Worcestershire, Shropshire and Herefordshire churches, and there are isolated instances elsewhere. In Essex there is an unparalleled group of wooden belfries, which are the ecclesiastical equivalent of the great barns scattered over the timber growing areas of England – an abandoned early-sixteenth-century example, St Mary, Mundon, was recently rescued by the Friends of Friendless Churches. There are also a few timber belfries in Herefordshire and Kent. A related curiosity is the unique timber bell-frame said to date from 1531, which stands in the churchyard of St Mary, East Bergholt, Suffolk.

It may seem perverse to start an account of church woodwork with a mention of these rarities, but this primacy is intentional. In the Middle Ages wood was a building material: in England, indeed, the carpenter had a longer tradition than the mason. An important carpenter was both engineer and architect, designing large and complex structures and overseeing their erection. Furthermore carpentry was essential to stone building; centering, templates, cranes, trestles and scaffolding were all made of wood. In recent years rapid progress has been made in understanding the history of wood construction. Archaeologists have organized timber-framed buildings into typological series; even the complex joints employed have been used for dating. Historians have used building accounts, wills and other documents to build up a picture of craftsmen and techniques. And, following research on the continent, the science of dendrochronology may soon provide secure dates to underpin the hitherto shaky foundations of knowledge.

While little survives of churches wholly of timber or framed in timber, and these survivals have, as a rule, a vernacular character – which gives a misleading impression of the status and capacity of the mediaeval 'church wright' – it would be very wrong to pretend that England's churches are poor in structural woodwork. On the contrary, this is one of their glories. To start at the entrance to the churchyard, the lych-gate is often an extremely neat piece of timberwork. Dating is difficult; both that at St James, Staple, in Kent, dated 1664, and that at St George, Clun, in Shropshire, dated 1723, look pre-Reformation. On rare occasions the lych-gate is elaborated into a timber-framed gate-house; that at St Michael, Bray, in Berkshire is dated 1448. Of porches there is a much richer legacy. They are usually of fairly basic construction, and often the main decorative interest lies in their barge-boards. These may have elaborate ogival cusping, as at St Mary, High Halden, in Kent (where the porch leads through an Essex-type timber belfry), which may be combined with blank panelled tracery, as at St Laurence, West Challow, in Berkshire. The occasional inscription may be found on a porch; that at St Mary & St Andrew, Whittlesford, in Cambridgeshire, records the name of the late-fifteenth-century donor, Henry Cyprian. The fourteenth-century north porch at St Mary, Boxford, in

139. Monkton Wyld, St Andrew, Dorset. Screen with rood by R. C. Carpenter, 1848–9

140. Detling, Kent; St Martin. Mid-fourteenth-century lectern

Suffolk, is perhaps the most remarkable in the country; its sides have traceried two-light windows, and its interior has a rib-vault with crisp, architectural mouldings.

The door through which a church is entered should not be overlooked. Early doors have plain boarding affixed to a second layer of boards or to a massive framework or grid of intersecting battens; their main decorative interest lies in elaborate applied ironwork, although Victorian architects found a fertile source of inspiration in the battening. From the mid-fourteenth century onwards applied mouldings gradually evolved into panelled construction. St Julian, Wellow, in Somerset has a head with blank reticulated tracery and six lights, St Mary, Stoke-by-Nayland, Suffolk, has a profusion of canopied niches containing figures, and the Greenway chapel at St Peter, Tiverton, in Devon, dating from 1517, has remarkable early Renaissance pilasters and ornament.

But the supreme splendours of structural woodwork in this country lie in the great timber roofs. Such is their variety and quantity that only a few examples of some different types can be cited. Suffolk is the great county for roofs, from the noble but structurally simple nave roof of Holy Trinity, Blythburgh, preserving much of its original polychromy and angels peppered with shot by William Dowsing's men in 1643, to the extraordinary complex aisled and clerestoried grandeur of that at St John the Baptist, Needham Market, soaring over the earthbound dullness of the nave. In Somerset St Peter & St Paul, Shepton Mallet, has a waggon roof with 350 panels encrusted with 350 different tracery patterns: other notable roofs of this type are in Devon, as at St Andrew, Cullompton. Cheshire possesses a splendid group with cambered tie-beams, and panelled decoration; those at St Mary, Astbury, have elaborate pendants, coated in delicate tracery. Until its demolition in 1960 Holy Trinity in Worcester contained the magnificent 1326 roof of the cathedral Guesten House, which is now the great treasure of the Avoncroft Museum of Buildings. At St Laurence, Ludlow, in Shropshire there is a fine wooden vault in the lofty late-fifteenth-century tower, and it should not be forgotten that most church spires are supported on a timber framework. The thirteenth-century lead-covered example at St Mary, Long Sutton, in Lincolnshire, is the oldest and largest in England.

In the Middle Ages almost every English church had a screen to separate the chancel, which belonged to the clergy, from the nave, the province of the laity, and on this screen, supported on a loft, or sometimes higher up on a rood beam, stood the rood. This has invariably been destroyed, nor do many rood lofts or beams survive. The

141. Fordingbridge, Hampshire; St Mary. Fifteenth-century North Chapel roof

chancel arch above and behind the rood was sometimes filled in, but few of these tympana are preserved. That at St Peter, Wenhaston, in Suffolk was discovered in 1892 when the whitewashed boards which composed it were left out in the churchyard and rain revealed a crudely painted Last Judgement. However the chancel screens themselves survive in their hundreds, and to these must be added a great quantity of parclose screens, which close off side chapels from chancel and aisles. The few remaining thirteenth-century wooden screens are simple: that at St Michael, Stanton Harcourt, in Oxfordshire has banded columns with trefoil tracery above. Decorated examples display an increasing elaboration: typical characteristics such as complex tracery patterns with multiple cusping, gables with crockets, and pinnacled buttresses, are conspicuous at St Margaret, Kings Lynn, in Norfolk. However, the real flowering of English screenwork took place in the fifteenth century. All vertical and horizontal members were elaborately moulded, panels and openings were headed with delicate tracery and the tops of screens had elaborate cresting or rich vaulted coving. In the latter case screens were usually arcaded, and often have only a vestigial fringe of cusping round their arches. Screens were painted and much original colour still survives, including

figures of saints in the panels of the dado. The quality is rarely so high as at St Edmund, Southwold, in Suffolk, where the screens are also encrusted with moulded and gilt *gesso* decoration. Although fine screens are to be found all over the country, the two richest areas are East Anglia and the South-West. At St George, Dunster, in Somerset the square-headed 1498 screen has a richly carved foliate frieze, while on the arcaded screen at St James, Swimbridge, in Devon every surface is coated with carved ornament of an almost coralline intricacy. In Suffolk the parclose screens of St Mary, Dennington, preserve their lofts, filling the arches at the eastern ends of aisles and nave with multiple tiers of filigree cresting and tracery, painted in bright colours.

Stalls are a common feature in many of the greater parish churches of England. A few have canopies like cathedral stalls: the Decorated examples at St Mary, Lancaster, are elaborately gabled, crocketed and traceried, while those at All Saints, Hereford, of about 1400, have projecting ogival arches, richly cusped and surmounted by a grille of tracery. The panelled fronts of the desks which stand before stalls are usually decorated with tracery, at its most elaborate at St Edmund, Southwold, in Suffolk, or sometimes with linenfold as at All Saints, Hillesden,

Buckinghamshire. The desk ends as a rule have poppy-head finials and are often supported by frontal buttresses surmounted by figures. At St Mary, Nosely, in Leicestershire, the stalls of 1473–4 bear bold cocks, the badge of the Staunton family. The ends themselves are most commonly carved with tracery, but often heraldry is employed, as in the 1528 stalls of Holy Trinity, Wensley, in Yorkshire, and occasionally figures of saints as at St Peter & St Paul, Barkestone, in Leicestershire. The stalls themselves almost invariably have a massive curved and moulded capping, projecting to form arm-rests. Beneath each arm-rest the stall is separated from its neighbours by standards, which usually have elbows decorated with a carved figure – birds and angels being popular motifs. The thirteenth-century stalls at St Mary, Kidlington, in Oxfordshire, have simple circular finials in this position.

Beneath the tip-up seats of the stalls are misericords, small ledges for support while in a standing position, usually decorated on their underside. Misericords have some of the most interesting and varied carving in English churches. Their quality ranges from the magnificent

142. Kenton, Devon; All Saints. Detail of fifteenth-century parclose screen

143. Stoke by Nayland, Suffolk; St Mary. Fifteenth-century south door

woodwoses at Holy Trinity, Coventry, and at St Katherine, Loversall, in Yorkshire, which are comparable to those in Lincoln Cathedral, to the simple rusticity of those at St Nicholas, Swineshead, Bedfordshire. Their subjects provide an index of mediaeval imagery from Reynard the fox to the strange creatures of the Bestiaries, from heraldry to grimacing grotesques. A special feature of English misericords, in contrast to continental examples, is the presence of supporters, small carvings flanking the central ledge. These add considerably to the formal and iconographic interest of misericords, and often display great ingenuity and charm. At St Botolph, Boston, in Lincolnshire, for example, a stag is flanked by a hound and a camel.

Naves may have been furnished with benches as early as the thirteenth century; simple examples which might be of this period survive at St Mark, Mark, in Somerset. But the vast majority of existing benches are fifteenth century or later, the main areas being East Anglia and the West Country. In East Anglia bench ends are usually surmounted by poppyheads and often flanked by buttresses bearing small figures. The ends and backs of benches may be filled with tracery, sometimes incorporating heraldry or religious emblems, or, rarely, figures. The elaborate set at St Mary, Wiggenhall St Mary, in Norfolk, combines all these features. Even the simpler East Anglian benches display a sense of architectural articulation, and the best, those at St

Peter & St Paul, Fressingfield, in Suffolk, are works of real refinement. This could rarely be said of West Country benches, but what these may lack in distinction they make up in vigour and invention. They are usually massive rectangular slabs of oak and the later examples, including a few as late as that at All Saints, Trull, in Somerset, signed Simon Werman and dated 1560, illustrate the naturalization of Renaissance motifs. Werman's name also occurs at All Saints, Broomfield, in Somerset, and at St Nonna, Altarnun, in Cornwall, a bench is inscribed 'Robart Daye, Maker of this Work', but nothing is known of the identities and careers of most mediaeval carvers.

At St Vigor, Fulbourn, in Cambridgeshire, is a wooden pulpit of the fourteenth century, which is polygonal with buttresses at its angles and arched heads to each of its open sides. Apart from these openings it anticipates the form of the mass of surviving mediaeval wooden pulpits, which date from the fifteenth century. The original support usually took the form of a slender shaft supporting a polygonal coving. As with other types of church woodwork the most elegant examples are in East Anglia and the most elaborate in the West Country. East Anglia also has many examples of painted decoration. Worthy of note elsewhere are the linenfold pulpit at St Michael, Heighington, in County Durham, inscribed with an injunction to pray for the donors, Alexander Flettcher and Agnes, his wife, and that at St Mary, Edlesborough, in Buckinghamshire (now redundant), which has the unique feature of a tall pinnacled tester.

Mediaeval font covers are relatively common, and their composition is often similar to that of the Edlesborough tester. But at St Mary, Ufford, in Suffolk is an eighteen-foot high font cover which beggars comparison: on 31 August 1643 the inconoclast Dowsing wrote, 'There is a glorious cover over the font, like a Pope's triple crown, a pelican on the top picking its breast, all gilt over with gold'. The gold has gone, but glorious it remains. At St Mary, Ewelme, in Oxfordshire, is another rich cover, presented by John, Duke of Suffolk, after the death of his mother in 1475, and St John, Halifax, in Yorkshire contains another fine example. Font covers were sometimes supported from the roof or a special beam, sometimes from a crane. A noble example of the latter device is at St Peter & St Paul, Salle, in Norfolk, where it projects from the gallery in the tower. It should also be mentioned that the occasional wooden font survives, as at St Andrew, Marks Tey, in Essex.

The Easter Sepulchre, in which a consecrated Host was reserved from Good Friday until Easter Sunday, was often of wood. But all have been destroyed, with the possible exception of a fine canopied chest at St Michael, Cowthorpe, in Yorkshire (now redundant). This object also resembles a tomb, and it should be remembered that tombs and effigies were sometimes of wood. At St John the

144. Noseley, Leicestershire; St Mary. Detail of stalls bearing the Staunton cock, about 1473–4

145. Iwerne Courtney, Dorset; St Mary. Seventeenth-century screen to the Freke chapel

Baptist, Danbury, in Essex are three effigies of knights of around 1400, while at St Mary, Staindrop, in County Durham is the remarkable Gothic monument by John Tarbotons to Henry Neville, Fifth Earl of Westmorland, who died in 1564. Mediaeval wooden lecterns have survived in some quantity, and two basic types may be distinguished, the eagle and the desk. Of the former that at All Saints, Leighton Buzzard, in Bedfordshire, is a good example, and of the latter that at St Martin, Detling, in Kent, the best. Among other small fittings alms boxes should be mentioned. They are usually crude iron-bound lumps of oak, but occasionally may be carved with tracery, as at Holy Trinity, Blythburgh, in Suffolk. Also in Suffolk, at St John Baptist, Barnby, is the only original door to a banner stave locker to have survived: it has crude pierced tracery and is more remarkable for its rarity than its quality. Pyx canopies are also exceedingly rare; the best is that at Milton Abbey in Dorset, while at St John the Evangelist, Warkleigh, in Devon, is a unique painted wooden box said to be a pyx case.

Of mediaeval wooden movables only chests remain, although in most cases movable is a misnomer for such massive objects. Primitive and undatable dug-outs are ubiquitous, often with a multiplicity of iron hinges and banding; a typical example is at St Cuthbert, Crayke, in Yorkshire. Early plank chests are sometimes decorated with chip-carved roundels, but Decorated chests may

146. Old Dilton, Wiltshire; St. Mary. Eighteenth-century furnishings

147. Rycote, Oxfordshire; St Michael. Wooden pews before the recent restoration

have elaborate tracery combined with beasts, as at All Saints, Wath-upon-Dearne, also in Yorkshire. Some later chests have applied tracery and buttresses, similar to contemporary screens: St Margaret, Huttoft, in Lincolnshire contains a celebrated example.

While the latter half of the sixteenth century is a blank period for church woodwork, the early seventeenth century is one of the most interesting. Gothic survived, or was revived, in such remarkable pieces as the 1618 screen at St Mary Magdalene, Geddington, and the 1628 stalls with misericords at St Guthlac, Passenham, both in Northamptonshire, and the 1612 benches with Jacobean poppyheads at St Mary, Bedingfield, in Suffolk. St Michael, Mere, in Wiltshire on the other hand has simple benches of 1638–41 in the northern Renaissance manner and St Mary, Croscombe, in Somerset has a towering and elaborate rood screen in the same style dated 1616. Pulpits were provided for many churches at this period: that at St Peter & St Paul, Aldeburgh, in Suffolk was made in 1632 after a trip by Charles Warne, the maker, to the neighbouring church of St Mary & St Peter, Kelsale, 'to see a pulpit', which also survives. At St Michael, Lyme Regis, in Dorset is a fine pulpit with a crested tester inscribed 'To God's Glory Richard Harvey of London Mercer and Marchant Adventurer 1613'. Jacobean font covers are sometimes very elaborate; that at St Mary, Mendlesham, in Suffolk, with a profusion of finials and pediments, was

ordered from John Turner, together with the pulpit, in 1630. Not only is the font cover Jacobean at St Denys, Stanford-in-the-Vale, in Berkshire, the font itself was encased in Jacobean panelling at the same time.

Altar rails were first introduced to most churches in the early seventeenth century: among the rare dated examples are those of 1625 at St Mary, Langley Marish, in Buckinghamshire, while those at St Mary, Troston, in Suffolk bear a scriptural inscription in Latin. Nearly all early altar tables are also of this period. At St Mary, Alne, in Yorkshire is a simple baluster-legged example dated 1628, and at St John, Leeds, in the same county, the richly carved table is contemporary with the rest of the furnishings of this remarkable church, supplied by Francis Gunby in 1632–4. Another feature introduced to churches at this date was the pew. At St Mary, Breedon-on-the-Hill, in Leicestershire, is the Shirley family pew, set up in 1627 and vaunting family pride in a lavish display of heraldry and cresting. The elaborate furnishings of the Chapel of St Michael, Rycote, in Oxfordshire include two monumental early seventeenth-century pews, one with a grand ogival canopy. However, the culminating monument of early-seventeenth-century church woodwork is the work of William Smith at Holy Trinity, Staunton Harold, in Leicestershire, commenced in 1653, completed in 1665, and amazingly untouched since.

Wren's City churches contain the most elaborate

148. Salwarpe, Worcestershire; St Michael. Chest dated 1697

149. St Hilary, Cornwall. William White, 1854. Structural timberwork

ecclesiastical woodwork of the late seventeenth century. Their country counterparts are not great in number. Robert Hooke's St Mary Magdalene, Willen, in Buckinghamshire retains its complete furnishings of 1679–80. St Genevieve, Euston, in Suffolk, has a beautiful reredos and other fittings in the metropolitan manner of about 1676, and Holy Trinity, Minsterley, in Shropshire, of 1689 represents a more rustic level of achievement. A surprising amount of city woodwork has strayed to country churches. The pulpit from St Margaret, Westminster, dated 1682, is now in St John the Baptist, Meopham, in Kent, and at St Mary Magdalene, Great Burstead, in Essex is the reredos from St Christopher le Stocks. St Lawrence, Great Waldingfield, in Suffolk has the communion rails from St Michael Cornhill, attributed to William Cleere. Another distinguished set of displaced communion rails are those from Wren's Pembroke College Chapel, Cambridge, now at St Mary, Tarrant Hinton, in Dorset.

A few unusual survivals are worthy of mention. At St Mary, Therfield, in Hertfordshire, is a cedar monument to Ann Turner († 1677). All Saints, Northampton, of 1676–80, contains a splendid mayoral chair dated 1680. Another fine mayoral chair, dated 1748, is at St Peter & St Paul, Blandford Forum, in Dorset. The dole cupboard presented by Jeremiah Bright of London to St Martin, Ruislip, in Middlesex, in 1697, is paralleled by that at St Peter, Coughton, in Warwickshire, 1717, and by another in the north porch of St Mary, Woodbridge, in Suffolk.

The eighteenth century has now been broached. Most fittings of this period have been swept away, both from mediaeval churches, and often from the few churches erected in the 1700s. As recently as 1965 the early-eighteenth-century galleries were removed from St Nicolas, Nuneaton, in Warwickshire. But there are survivals, and many of these are in delightful, remote, country churches, such as All Saints, Chalbury, and St Andrew, Winterborne Tomson, both in Dorset, St Oswald, Ravenstonedale, in Westmorland, St Mary, Old Dilton, in Wiltshire, and St Mary, Monnington-on-Wye, in Herefordshire. Some very fine eighteenth-century ensembles also survive in meeting houses and chapels. Joseph Clarke's Unitarian Meeting House of 1699 to 1700, Ipswich, in Suffolk, contains a superb pulpit, pews and galleries; a simpler example is the Congregational Chapel of 1757 at Garrigill in Cumberland. Also in Cumberland St James, Whitehaven, built in 1752–3 is a grand classical interior intact. Its Rococo Gothic contemporary is Bateman's refurnishings of St John the Evangelist, Shobdon, in Herefordshire, also of 1753. The grand Neo-classical manner is represented by Thomas Hardwick's St Mary, Wanstead, in Essex, of 1787–90.

Early nineteenth-century church woodwork was frequently replaced later in that century, and little of what survives attracts particular notice now. Exceptions are Francis Goodwin's organ case of 1822 at Holy Trinity, Bordesley, in Warwickshire, and the strange naturalistic works of Sarah Losh at St Mary, Wreay, in Cumberland. One important development from the 1820s onwards was the growth of a practice of importing carving and furniture of all kinds from both continental and native sources, and using them to beautify churches. Notable antiquarian confections of this type are St Leonard, Old Warden, in Bedfordshire, assembled by Lord Ongley in about 1841 and St Catherine, Birtles, in Cheshire, collected by Thomas Hibbert in about 1840. But there are few churches which do not possess some fragment of antiquity of this stamp, be it a chair, a chest or a woodcarving. All too often, alas, their provenance and donor are fogotten. Such is the case with the set of mid-eighteenth-century ladderback chairs at St Mary, Newport, in Essex, one of which was recently discovered to bear the label of Giles Grendey, and which is now on loan to the Victoria & Albert Museum.

Pugin, Butterfield, Street, Pearson, Bodley, Comper – the list could easily be extended – all the major church architects of the nineteenth century took a close and personal interest in the design of church fittings, not only for their own churches, but also for those which they restored. Much has been mutilated: Pugin's organ of about 1849 for St Mary, West Tofts, in Norfolk, now at nearby All Saints, South Pickenham, is sundered from its gallery. And much is lost: the tragic demolition of Norman Shaw's Holy Trinity, Bingley, in Yorkshire, of 1866–8 is fresh in the memory. But numerous splendid ensembles do survive, from Teulon's remote St James, Hunstanworth, in County Durham, of 1863, to Pearson's noble St Mary, Freeland, in Oxfordshire, of 1871. Nor should the

pious and sometimes charming works of reverend amateurs be forgotten. The 1896 screen at St John Evangelist, Windermere, in Westmorland is by the vicar, E. S. Robertson, and his parishioners, and that at Littlebury, in Essex was erected by Rev. H. J. Burell in 1911. St Nicholas, Bulwick, Northamptonshire, contains a run of benches by J. H. Holdich, vicar from 1862–92, while St Peter, Plemstall, in Cheshire, is bedecked with carving by J. H. Toogood, incumbent from 1907–46. Local landowners have also contributed. St Nicholas, Rushbrooke, in Suffolk, is a showplace of the 1840-ish carvings of Colonel Rushbrooke, and the late-nineteenth-century pulpit of All Saints, Laxton, in Northamptonshire, is by Lord Carbery.

It is difficult in a brief account of a vast subject to draw the balance between the anthology of masterpieces and the pot-pourri of the curious and the typical, and even more so to include all that is important or relevant. Royal arms, collecting shoes, biers, clock jacks, grave boards, and pulpit tester tables are among the casualties. At the beginning of this essay the physical vulnerability of wood was stressed. Despite this great riches have survived in the churches of this country; it is to be hoped that through knowledge and appreciation, piety and humility, they may be defended from their perennial enemies, more insidious than any physical threats, ignorance and philistinism, impiety and arrogance.

150. London, Stepney; St George's Lutheran Church. Interior woodwork, 1762–3

STAINED GLASS
by Martin Harrison

A conservative estimate of the number of stained glass windows still extant in our churches would give a figure in the region of 80,000: our legacy is both rich and enormous. But the number is, perhaps permanently, continually decreasing, and the alarming predictions of church redundancies expected in the immediate future will see a further growth in the problem. In order to understand the situation more clearly, first let us examine the question of the distribution, chronologically and geographically, of stained glass in Britain.

Stained glass dating from earlier than 1840 is extremely rare in Scottish churches, and never indigenous; in Wales it is confined largely to the north-east, and again is scarce enough to present, in terms of the volume to be preserved, no great problems. So it will be clear that, as far as the future of pre-Victorian stained glass is endangered, the problem exists in England alone, where it is further confined almost entirely to Anglican churches and cathedrals. With the notable exceptions of York and Canterbury our cathedrals no longer possess extensive series of mediaeval glazing, and this in itself is the result of earlier destruction, which has been well charted. The loss of so much of our mediaeval stained glass was formerly blamed almost exclusively on the Reformation but it has since been shown that equally disastrous were the subsequent centuries of ignorance and neglect. Whilst one cannot imagine deliberate inconoclasm being responsible for the loss of further ancient glass in the foreseeable future, we must take every precaution not to lay ourselves open to future claims of neglect or ignorance. Our great heritage of mediaeval stained glass – one of the major art forms of its time – can still be found to a considerable extent in parish churches, and it is in these that the potential causes for alarm lie. For example, the kind of situation one meets with far too often is a remote rural church which contains, in a completely unprotected tracery light, an exquisite fourteenth-century figure; behind the glass a bird has been allowed to nest, attaching the nest to trailing ivy or a rusting fragment of wire guard, or a vandal has decided to take a pot-shot with a stone or pellet – in either case the results can mean damage which both lessens the quality of the glass and is far more costly than proper protection would have been.

Despite this the amount of mediaeval and other stained glass made before 1840 likely to be rendered homeless is, for some years at least, relatively small. Windows whose future might otherwise have been threatened (e.g. the fourteenth-century glass from Hadzor Church, Worcestershire) are catered for by the Stained Glass Museum, founded in 1972 and located at Ely Cathedral, which exists to preserve and display fine stained glass of all periods, and which will certainly be able to cope with all redundant pre-Victorian glass for some years. To summarize, the problem with earlier glass in our parish churches is not so much the threat of possible redundancy but one of either neglect or, as is often the case, a genuine desire to maintain and protect the glass without the financial means to do so.

The York Glaziers Trust was set up jointly by the dean and chapter and the Pilgrim Trust in 1967; a permanent team of glaziers attached to the minster had already long been established, but the formation of the Trust, and recognition of its status as a charity, was an important step, especially since the Trust has now been able to expand its sphere of activities and carry out repair work for many other churches on glass of all periods. A similar workshop has been more recently set up at Canterbury with the principal object of saving from further decay the great wealth of stained glass for which the Cathedral is justly renowned. A long-established and highly experienced workshop, specializing in the conservation of stained glass,

151. Newton in the Willows, Northamptonshire; St Faith. The east window, by Clayton & Bell, 1858, photographed in 1972, prior to the church's conversion into a field studies centre. The problems of vandalism can be acute in a remote rural church and every window here was destroyed

is run by Mr Dennis King in Norwich, and to this group must be added the Corpus Vitrearum, the international body for the recording and conservation of stained glass, whose Comité Technique, headed in England by Professor Roy Newton of the University of York, regularly issues a stimulating *News Letter* for the discussion and dissemination of information regarding the latest conservation techniques.

Stained and painted glass dating from between 1550 and 1840 is extremely rare, and it would seem essential that all windows from this period should be preserved on grounds of scarcity alone. Their value further lies in the fact that they show the continuity of the medium throughout those years when, though undoubtedly in decline, the art of stained glass – contrary to frequent mistaken assertions – never died out in England. The pictorially conceived productions of the seventeenth and eighteenth centuries have suffered probably even greater abuse than their Victorian counterparts, and perhaps it would be apposite to make a plea here for their better understanding. The problem for most critics seems to be that windows of the seventeenth and eighteenth centuries are so clearly the very antithesis of their great mediaeval predecessors such as the glass at Chartres or Canterbury. Of course this is quite true, and especially so of the Georgian period when not only was most of the glass used simply clear sheet glass which was painted with coloured enamels but the function of the lead-lines seemed to have been ignored in favour of placing the glass panes in a simple, regular framework of rectangular patterns. The great mistake is to suppose that these later artists were attempting to emulate the styles of their twelfth- and thirteenth-century forebears. Seen in the context of their own time their work often appears quite remarkable and achieves effects in stained glass never attempted before or since.

In the first half of the seventeenth century the leading stained glass artists in England were the Dutch Van Linge brothers, Bernard and Abraham, and though much of their work has been lost to subsequent changes in fashion a fair amount still survives, principally in the Oxford college chapels. Henry Gyles of York was the most eminent glass painter in the latter part of the seventeenth century, and again a number of his windows, mostly heraldic, still remain. The Price family, William the Elder, Joshua, and William the Younger, made many notable windows in the late seventeenth and early eighteenth centuries, including two still to be seen in Westminster Abbey, the north transept rose window of 1723 and the great west window of 1735. In 1702 William Price the Elder had made the large east window of Merton College Chapel, Oxford; this was

removed in the inter-war period – a time when the reputation of such windows was at its lowest ebb – but was fortunately placed in store rather than destroyed. It has recently been loaned to the Ely Stained Glass Museum and will shortly be placed on show there.

Some of the major monuments of the post-mediaeval pre-Victorian period in stained glass were the direct outcome of the Romantic Movement and the revived taste for the Gothick style. James Pearson's striking 'Moses and the Brazen Serpent' still fortunately adorns Salisbury Cathedral, and Thomas Jervais's west window, designed by Sir Joshua Reynolds, survives at New College, Oxford, where there is also work by William Peckitt of York. Finally two major examples by Francis Eginton of Birmingham should be mentioned, the east window of St Alkmund's, Shrewsbury, and the stunningly dramatic east window of St Paul's, Birmingham, the latter designed by Sir Benjamin West.

Comparatively speaking, however, only a minute amount of this sort of painted glass exists, and only on referring to contemporary accounts does the extent of the Georgian revival of glass painting become apparent. The Victorians' zeal for Gothicizing their churches swept away much of this glass, which was considered theatrical and pagan, and important losses were later sustained in the two World Wars, including the series at Lincoln's Inn Chapel by the Van Linges and the east window of St Leonard's, Shoreditch, dating from 1634 – the most important surviving window by Baptista Sutton. It is to be hoped that henceforth the few score of specimens of painted glass which we still have will be jealously safeguarded.

In my opening remarks I hazarded an estimate that a total of 80,000 windows existed in England, Scotland and Wales. If one carries this one stage further to suggest that 90 per cent of that total is made up of windows dating from later than 1840, it will be clear that a massive problem for the future is posed by the vast amount of stained glass made in the Victorian, Edwardian and modern periods.

The nineteenth century was hardly over before quite considerable amounts of early Victorian stained glass had been replaced by more recent work. A typical example of this was the replacement of Ward and Nixon's south transept window in Westminster Abbey. Placed in 1847, it was pronounced by the eminent antiquary and promoter of the revival of stained glass, Charles Winston, to be 'the first English work in which any attempt to carry out a legitimate system of glass painting has been made' and he spoke of its 'superiority over its contemporaries, both here and abroad'. In 1902, the barely less eminent writer and stained glass artist Lewis F. Day thought it a 'gaudy

152. Claygate, Surrey; Holy Trinity. Three superb windows by Heaton, Butler & Bayne were rendered virtually meaningless by removal of their backgrounds and insensitive releading of the subject sections. Shown here, a detail of one of the lights as treated in 1974

153. Hadzor, Worcestershire; St John the Baptist. Declared redundant and sold for an alternative use in 1976. The fine fourteenth-century glass was rescued by the Ely Stained Glass Museum

154. Dedworth, Berkshire; All Saints. During demolition. This small but attractive church by Bodley which contained a full set of Morris glass, 1863–88, had to be demolished because of its structural condition. The glass was saved for re-use

155. Youlgreave, Derbyshire; All Saints. A major east window designed by Sir Edward Burne-Jones and made by William Morris & Co. in 1876, cleaned with a harsh cleansing powder by a film company to 'make it lighter'. The result is an eating-away of the paint

horror' and this is a pretty accurate reflection of the Edwardian reaction to High Victorian intensity. In the event, in 1902 the Ward and Nixon window was replaced by an example of the work of Messrs Burlison and Grylls which now appears simply very dull.

Despite many similar losses the High Victorian period represents the absolute peak, in terms of quantity, of stained glass production. At this time, when the Gothic revival and concomitant popularity of darkly glowing, mystical interiors was at its height, it could not have been foreseen that the early years of the twentieth century and the advent of the Liturgical Movement would bring with them a demand for the return to lightened and white-washed church interiors. This spelled doom for much Victorian stained glass, and its repercussions are still prevalent in some quarters – even now the disastrous practice of removing Victorian figure subjects from their

156. Redbourne, Lincolnshire; St Andrew. Glass by Danby, depicting *Sodom and Gomorrah*

original setting and rendering them virtually meaningless by suspending them on clear backgrounds still persists, and is an unfortunate hangover from the 1920s when it was an officially approved method of lightening interiors. This practice is especially unfortunate since, as A. Charles Sewter writing in *Apollo* for December 1962 so astutely observed, 'it is often the case that the best parts of Victorian windows are the pattern-work panels, canopies and borders'. Prejudice against the nineteenth century is at last receding, but where ignorance still prevails irreparable harm has been done. How often one reads in a church guide an entry similar to this from a very recent guide to a small country church in Sussex: 'We are very fond of our stained glass but it is all Victorian and therefore, we are told, of no value.' Too often also, in a time of financial stringency, one still hears of old stained glass windows being removed and replaced by either costly plain glazing or – even more expensive – new stained glass.

But even more daunting is the spectre of the great increase in the number of threatened redundancies, which again, for obvious reasons, hits Victorian churches the hardest. The immediate solution, if we are not to lose more of our priceless and irreplaceable heritage, is for all stained glass that might otherwise be destroyed to be recorded and vetted: this is to some extent being achieved by the Ely Stained Glass Museum which, since its inception in 1972, has rescued many notable examples of stained glass from all periods. A long-term answer is more difficult to provide; perhaps the chief hope is that individual churches may be persuaded to utilize some of the profits arising from the sale of their properties to subsidize the expert removal of any important stained glass contained therein. This applies especially to denominations outside the Church of England, whose arrangements generally for dealing with redundant churches and their fittings tend to be somewhat haphazard. At least there are now real signs that the appreciation of stained glass is once again increasing: a sympathetic understanding of the special problems posed by the preservation of stained glass should ensure for it a safer future.

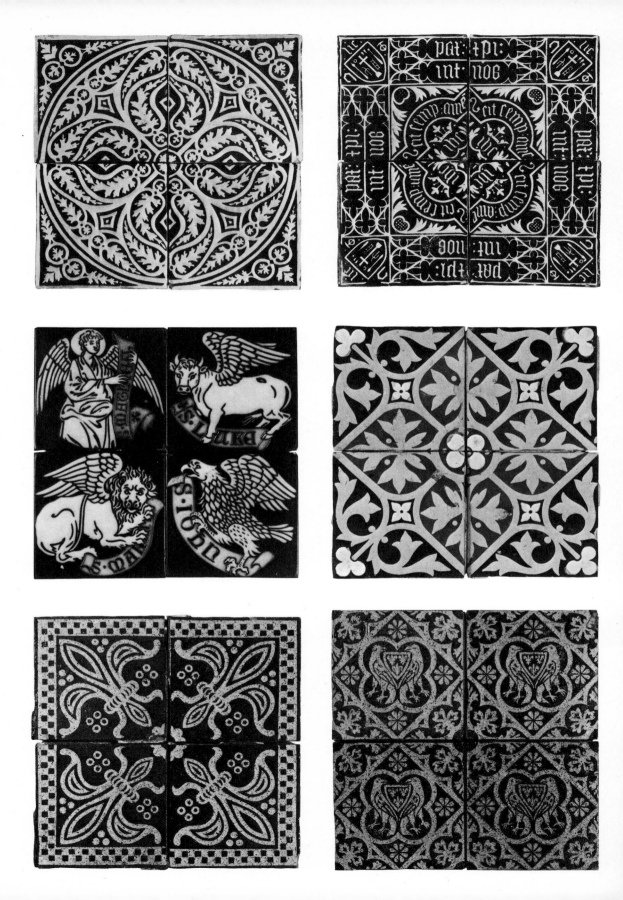

CERAMICS
by Michael Archer

In common with wood, metal and stone, clay has always played an important part in the construction of churches, but with the exception of floor and dado tiles it has had a strictly utilitarian role with little decorative application. Hardly any ecclesiastical equipment seems to have been made of pottery or porcelain, although candlesticks do exist which were designed in a Gothic idiom and may have been intended for church use. There are, too, a number of stem cups, a little like chalices, made in the nineteenth century with silver or copper lustre glazes, which are said to have been used in Nonconformist chapels. There is a good collection of these in the Welsh Folk Museum at St Fagan's Castle. Also of Methodist origin are the 'Love-feast' cups, in use between about 1830 and 1880, which are sometimes found inscribed with the names of chapels. Of more definite liturgical purpose are two categories of ceramic font. A group of four fonts exists made of Wedgwood black basalt. One of these, now at the Lady Lever Art Gallery, Port Sunlight, Merseyside, was given by Josiah Wedgwood to St Margaret Moreton Say, Shropshire, in 1783. The other three were given in 1778, 1783 and about 1786 to the Bedfordshire parish

churches of Essendon, Cardington and Melchbourne respectively by Mary, Harriet and Emma Whitbread, daughters of Samuel Whitbread. The Melchbourne font is no longer in the church and seems likely to be the one in the Buten Museum of Wedgwood at Merion, Pennsylvania. Fortunately none of the four basalt fonts has been destroyed, although it is a pity that only two remain in their original settings.

On a comparable scale is a bizarre salt-glazed stoneware font of the second half of the nineteenth century at St Peter and St Edward, Westminster, probably made by Doultons, who are known to have exhibited a similar object at the Philadelphia Centennial Exhibition of 1876. The bowl is incised to resemble a fisherman's net while water lilies decorate the top.

Much smaller are the far more numerous portable fonts of the nineteenth century. These were made of a fine white porcellaneous material with a smear glaze. It is known that they were specifically intended for use in churches, as is made clear by an author writing in 1842. 'A portable vase of white Wedgwood ware, with a cover to it; which can be set on a communion table when there is a baptism; and under it when not wanted.' A Minton pattern book of the late nineteenth century shows four models which they made, ranging in height from about six to sixteen inches. Generally they are precise copies of mediaeval stone fonts and the names of the churches where these original exemplars are to be found, such as 'St Mary's, Notts', are inscribed on the underside within a small, applied, decorative cartouche.

They may have been made by a number of different manufacturers and certainly first appeared in the 1840s. The Cambridge Camden Society, as part of its campaign to improve the design of churches and their contents, issued a pamphlet entitled *A Few Words to Church*

157, 158. Two groups of tiles made of buff and full red clay. Marked 'Chamberlain and Co, Worcester', *c.* 1839, 15 cm square. Victoria and Albert Museum

159. The signs of the Evangelists. White and buff colouring on a blue ground. Probably designed by A. W. N. Pugin. Marked 'Minton and Co', *c.* 1850, 15 cm

160. A group of four tiles decorated in buff and white on black and dull-red. Marked 'Campbell Brick and Tile Co'. Mid-nineteenth-century, 15 cm square. Victoria and Albert Museum

161, 162. Two groups of tiles in buff or brown, bearing the mark of W. Godwin of Lugwardine, Herefordshire. Third quarter of the nineteenth-century, 12.7 cm square. Victoria and Albert Museum

Builders with an appendix containing lists of windows, fonts and roodscreens intended to serve as models in 1841. The Camden Society seems to have been formulating a list of preferred font types at least as early as 1839 since there is a group of miniature copies made for them between that year and 1850. These are signed 'J Flack' and are now in the Yorkshire Museum, York. They are made of plaster with the most scrupulous eye for detail and are inscribed with the location of the exemplar. It is highly likely that the commercially produced ceramic fonts were made shortly after this date, betraying the influence of the Camden Society in their precise copying of mediaeval prototypes.

Fonts of this type are frequently alienated from the churches for which they were bought, largely because it is not appreciated that they were intended to be part of the permanent equipment, since stone fonts were not always installed when a church was built. They were recommended as inexpensive substitutes for stone ones. The Reverend Wilson is quoted in the *Architectural Magazine* of 1836 as saying, 'A very neat portable font has been given to the new church at Stonyhurst, which answers every purpose; not requiring even the expense of a stand; as it might be placed, when wanted, on the communion table, from which the ceremony might be performed. The price is fourteen shillings; and it is to be had at Sharpur's, Pall Mall East, London.'

The only other type of ceramic vessel intended for a church-related activity is the bell-ringers' 'gotch'. These are large jugs made to hold beer. They very rarely have any appropriate decoration and only proclaim their purpose through incised inscriptions. An exception is the superb stoneware jug at Sts Peter and Paul, Clare, Suffolk, which has a crisply modelled bell in relief on the shoulder. It is inscribed 'Clare Ringers, 1729'.

By far the most important visible use of clay in churches is in brick and tile floors and, to a lesser extent, in tiled dadoes. A surprising number of mediaeval parish churches still possess the remains of contemporary tiled floors. These are rarely more than small areas of broken and jumbled tiles but often possess considerable charm besides their historical importance. Far more common are the nineteenth-century copies of encaustic type. As early as 1830 Samuel Wright of Shelton in Staffordshire took out a patent for their manufacture. Three years later mediaeval tiles and kilns were found at Malvern in Herefordshire, and shortly afterwards the Worcester porcelain factory began to make clay tiles in the mediaeval manner. These were used by a local architect, Harvey Eginton, in church restoration work. In 1840 the restoration of the Temple church led to excavations which resulted in the discovery of mediaeval tiles. The replacement of these was undertaken by Minton & Co. of Stoke-on-Trent who soon became pre-eminent in the field. Other leading manufactures were Godwin of Lugwardine, Copelands, the Campbell Tile Co. and St John, Barr of Worcester, who took over Chamberlain's and were in turn to become Maw & Co.

Although at first sight very similar, the products of these firms could differ considerably. They all followed mediaeval prototypes closely but also made tiles to the design of architects. Often the lay-out of mediaeval floors was copied precisely, but great originality was also shown in the arrangement of groups to make great carpets of intricate patterns such as those in the House of Lords and at St David's Cathedral.

Ever since the late nineteenth century there has been controversy about Victorian encaustic tiles and they still arouse strong feelings. In *English Parish Churches as Works of Art*, Alec Clifton Taylor has written of them as 'characterized by a hard efficiency and a relentless precision'. Although this can be true of some types, there are others, notably the products of Chamberlain and of Godwin, which possess variety and texture as well as the capacity to wear attractively. Unfortunately the occasional church where the more strident type of encaustic tile has been used insensitively has led to considerable prejudice. Clifton Taylor goes on to say 'The removal of these "lavatory tiles" would not be a very costly matter, and it should be done all over the country'. Fortunately this recommendation is unlikely to be widely adopted, although there have been regrettable losses, such as the tiles from St Winefrid's, Shepshed, Leicestershire (built by Pugin) and the Godwin pavement from the choir of Salisbury Cathedral. The recent re-appraisal of Victorian art has opened many eyes to the crisp, formal qualities of encaustic tiles, many of which show considerable originality and even humour. The works of great designers such as Pugin and Willement are being disentangled from the mediaeval copies with which they are often confused and seen to be important manifestations of nineteenth-century decoration. Sometimes, too, a floor of encaustic tiles has historic value where it is a copy of a mediaeval original which has vanished or become indecipherable since the mid-nineteenth century. Examples of this are some Minton tiles made for the old Benedictine abbey church of Sherborne in Dorset which were the only means of discovering the pattern used on the mediaeval Wessex tiles of which they were copies.

Unfortunately church floors frequently suffer in a way

163. Font of porcellaneous earthenware with a smear glaze, inscribed on the underside 'St Mary Mag Oxford'. Unmarked but probably made by Minton & Co., *c.* 1840, height 33 cm. Private Collection

164. Tiles in dark brown and buff, possibly made by W. Godwin of Lugwardine, Herefordshire. Third quarter of the nineteenth-century, 11.4 cm square. Victoria and Albert Museum

that roofs or windows rarely do – they are altered piecemeal. There are various common reasons for this. Most floors are hardly ever seen in a large area uncovered or uncluttered. Often there is too much furniture, and a carpet can sometimes diminish the visual effect of a floor disastrously. A red carpet in the chancel at Chadshunt, near Banbury, Oxfordshire for example, so distracts the eye that one barely realizes that it lies on a fine black and white chequered floor. Because floors have frequently been treated piecemeal in small areas, there is a tendency for this process to continue. At its most attractive the effect can be highly picturesque with the charm of odd juxtapositions of form and texture. The chancel at Thaxted, Essex has a wide expanse of mixed brick, ledger stones and brasses which is delightful. Such an effect often goes unappreciated, particularly by those who have to clean it. The result is either dirt and neglect or a demand for a more easily maintained floor surface. In both cases the floor suffers. (Problems concerning the maintenance of churchyards are closely comparable. In the one case floors are 'tidied up', in the other monuments are removed or flattened.)

Another threat to floors, and one that has become particularly prevalent, is the moving of pews. Rows of unfilled pews can appear discouraging to a shrinking congregation. This sometimes leads to a re-ordering of churches as does the demand for space in which to carry out all the other activities for which they are increasingly used. When pews are removed it is often found that they stood on wooden staging which covers the floor surface beneath. Sometimes this is uneven or unsuitable in some other way for chairs and so the floor is altered.

But perhaps the greatest threat to floors is posed by the fact that most people are unaware of them. We tend to ignore them unless they are spectacular in some way. The fish let into the modern chancel floor of St Leonard's parish church in Sussex are unlikely to pass unnoticed, but there must be many who visit Great Offley near Hitchin, Hertfordshire who do not appreciate the superb black marble floor of the chancel or the simple pattern of red and black clay tiles in the nave, both mercifully free of carpet. Even less likely to be noticed is the fine brick floor in the porch. All these floors help to define the internal architectural spaces and emphasize the different uses to which they are put. But above all they are crucial to the atmosphere of the place. So many churches which may in other respects appear attractive or even actually beautiful can be unpleasant places to be in because of ugly floors.

ORGANS
by Michael Gillingham

The most expensive, the largest, and all too often the ugliest, of the church's furnishings is the organ. Is such a cumbrous machine really needed in the worship of God? Some Christians (notably the Scottish Presbyterians) have in the past forbidden the use of organs, believing that they ministered only to the pride of the flesh. In the Church of England changes in religious opinion have caused more destruction of organs than changes in architectural or liturgical fashion.

Before the mid-nineteenth century many an Anglican church, especially in the country, did not possess an organ. A band of woodwind and string players might have led the psalmody. Some churches had barrel-organs, mostly of early-nineteenth-century date. A few of these also had keyboards. In the cathedrals and prosperous town churches organs of some musical pretensions can be found, but few earlier in date than 1640.

Organs in mediaeval England were small and portative, even in the greater churches. A late-sixteenth-century account records the existence, in pre-Reformation times, of an organ in Durham Cathedral with an elaborately decorated case; and remarks that the only cathedrals to have anything comparable were York and St Paul's. The earliest organ-case now surviving in Britain is at St Stephen, Old Radnor, on the Welsh border, dating from *c.* 1525. The remoteness of its home probably saved it from destruction or sale – fates suffered by so many organs later in the reign of Elizabeth when Puritanism nearly succeeded in forbidding the use of organs altogether. Of the organ-cases traditionally ascribed to the sixteenth century, the smaller of the two at Gloucester Cathedral may perhaps on stylistic grounds be dated so; but the 'Milton' organ-case at Tewkesbury Abbey and the beautiful case at Stanford-on-Avon almost certainly date from the revival of church music under Archbishop Laud.

The Puritans objected particularly to the elaboration of music which organs made possible, and in 1644 an Order in Council commanded that 'all organs, and the frames or cases wherein they stand in all churches and chappells . . . shall be taken away and utterly defaced and none hereafter set up in their place'. So wholesale was the destruction that on 8 July 1660, Samuel Pepys could record hearing at the Chapel Royal in Whitehall 'organs and singing-men' for the first time in his life – at the age of twenty-eight.

Only seven organ-cases now remain which are thought to date from before 1660, and in none of them does a recognizable instrument of the period survive. Though this is sad for history's sake, the musical loss may not be so great, since the British organ was a stunted creature throughout Stuart and Georgian times compared with its brethren in Germany, Scandinavia, the Low Countries and France. Lacking a pedal keyboard, and often with not much variety of chorus-work on the manuals, it was unsuitable for the music of the great European composers. Compared with such music, the organ voluntaries enjoyed by Georgian congregations seem trite, and their solemn movements sound pedestrian. The musical resources of these organs were limited, but the more lavish works of such builders as Smith, the Harrisses, Bridge and the Byfields could be brilliant and extremely colourful, reflecting the traditions of those countries where Smith and Harris had spent the lean years of the Commonwealth. Their organ-cases from 1660 to 1730, with graceful outlines and rich decoration in carving, painting and gilding, were seemly ornaments, although Victorian ecclesiologists often found them somewhat pagan in taste.

The shapely form of the old style, in which the upper part containing the pipes overhung on each side the lower part which contained the keyboards and bellows, was forsaken by later eighteenth-century builders, whose box-like cases

165. Old Radnor, Radnorshire; St Stephen. Early sixteenth-century case restored and fitted with new organ in 1873

relied for comeliness on the excellence of cabinet-work, carving and expensive inlay. The Gothic style might be used, following the published designs of Chippendale; but only skin-deep, as an alternative to a thin version of the classical orders. It degenerated too easily, to quote Sir John Sutton writing in 1847, into 'innumerable pinnacles' like 'the barley-sugar ornaments we see about Christmas time in pastry-cooks' windows'.

Sutton was at the centre of the ecclesiological movement: an ally of Pugin, and with friends and brothers (including F. H. Sutton) in holy orders, who furnished their churches with organ-cases in correct revived Gothic. Perhaps the most beautiful of all to have survived is that in South Pickenham church, Norfolk, formerly (with its tribune) in West Tofts church nearby.

Many of the later Gothic revival architects disliked the seventeenth- and eighteenth-century classical organ-cases, especially in parish churches. The west gallery organs were a particular nuisance. They might move east, following the choir to the chancel, but to squeeze them into organ chambers, or under low aisle roofs, cornices had to be lopped and tower caps shorn away. The invention of pneumatic and, later, electrical mechanisms that enabled the keyboards to operate more pipes with less effort, and from a longer distance than was possible under the discipline of the old 'tracker' action, encouraged excesses in tone and untidiness in layout, and quite destroyed the architectural unity of the instrument.

Among the architects, Bodley designed some beautiful cases in a true Gothic spirit, much influenced and often advised by F. H. Sutton, as at Hoar Cross, Staffordshire. The Gothic cases of Sir Gilbert Scott, R. C. Carpenter, Temple Moore, W. D. Caroë, and the organ-builder A. G. Hill, and those by Sir Thomas Jackson in the classical style, were all handsome church ornaments, but acted as a decorative screen rather than an expression of the musical architecture of the instrument. This weakness is carried to extreme in the pretty cases of Sir Ninian Comper where the scale of the display pipes (which rarely speak) bears no relation to that of the organ within. The result of breaking the old unity of organ and case was the familiar sight of naked grey pipes supported by more or less decent panelling.

Churches are dismayed at the cost of keeping up these memorials. Gone are the days of well-attended organ recitals, and the dignified congregation at Choral Matins has given place to more relaxed families at the Parish Communion. However, during the last twenty years many church musicians have re-discovered the virtues of old organs from pre-pneumatic days, inspired by the re-storation of Georgian survivals. Many a modest Victorian organ has come back to life as organists recognize that a few stops clearly voiced and strategically placed will lead a congregation better than thrice the number buried in a chamber.

The case for preserving these organs may seem well proved, but far too many are still lost because the organist wants something larger, with more devices to help him play, or electric action so that he can be far away from the noise he makes. Even organs of acknowledged historic importance are not safe from alteration. 'Minor changes, to bring the instrument in line with current tonal ideas' is a death-knell too often heard, and it usually means that the character of the organ will be irrevocably spoilt. Such works have sometimes been done in defiance of the faculty jurisdiction, and against expert advice. Ruining the achievement of an artist organ-builder to satisfy the present incumbent of the organ-stool is inexcusable.

The fate of late Victorian and Edwardian organs in the Romantic style is sadly uncertain. Those by the best builders are works of art in their own right, with orchestral and ethereal stops of great beauty. In prosperous churches they often fall victim to the tinkering organist who persuades a builder to add so-called Baroque registers, voiced (if genuine) in an utterly different style, vainly hoping that some sort of classical organ will be the result. In churches likely to become redundant, the large Romantic organs are an embarrassment – costly and difficult to store and re-house. If a redundant church is demolished, such an organ usually suffers the same fate or becomes a quarry for the local organ-builder.

There are two problems we must solve. The first is the proper treatment of our historic organs. They must be listed, fully described and protected. Not only the pre-Victorian organs and organ-cases but the untouched works of Victorian and Edwardian builders must be safeguarded against ignorant alteration masquerading as restoration. We have to accept a history of rebuilding which may mean that the remains of a seventeenth- or eighteenth-century scheme are enshrined in later work which should be kept, if at all sympathetic, in the same spirit as are the later additions to a mediaeval church.

The second problem is to persuade organists and church authorities to see the virtues of an instrument which the player can control directly by the music of his fingers. The discipline of size, shape and layout in which the key action unites the organist by tracker to his pipes is not merely an antiquarian notion; it has the beauty of economy, and it makes the organ a living work of musical art, a true instrument of worship.

CHURCHYARDS
by Pamela Burgess

The churchyards which nestle around our parish churches and the gravestones which were set up to mark the burial places of past parishioners probably form the largest and most neglected area of our archaeological and architectural heritage.

The study of gravestones is regarded by many as a morbid occupation and yet these same people, who will tread delicately, almost fearfully, around the graves in a churchyard, will walk boldly over the memorial ledgers covering the church floor, apparently oblivious of the fact that these too cover interments. Brass rubbing has been for many years a popular hobby and is never regarded as morbid. Perhaps these enthusiasts do not associate brasses with death.

It is only in recent years that churchyards have become regarded as gloomy places, and one assumes that this is the outcome of loss of faith and the resultant fear of death. Past records show that the churchyard was once the focal point of village life – a place where meetings could be held and games played. Literature reveals that a walk among the tombstones was an acceptable and pleasant pastime in the nineteenth century, and the many books of epitaphs published at that time support this. The epitaphs themselves often refer to this diversion. Many refer to 'Reader' or 'Passer-by'. The epitaph to Francis Davis, soap-boiler, of Leominster, Herefordshire, who died in 1834 tells of his personal perambulations:

'Often I've walked this Church Yard round
And viewed the names of those I knew.
And by reflections force I found
That I must die as well as you.'

Many poets found inspiration in churchyards, the most famous being Thomas Gray. Thomas Hardy deplored the tidying-up of churchyards in his poem 'The Levelled Churchyard':

'Where we are huddled none can trace,
And if our names remain,
They pave some path or porch or place,
Where we have never lain.'

When studying the history of churches and churchyards one is confronted with the same vexed question as that of the chicken and the egg. Where were Christians buried before there were churches and churchyards in which to bury them?

In the sixth century a decree of Justinian specified that a cross should precede the building of a church, and the setting up of crosses continued throughout the mediaeval period. Is it not reasonable to assume that Christians were buried within the vicinity of the cross? Many churchyards still contain fragments of early crosses, and I personally believe that most churchyards pre-date the churches which they surround.

The setting up of individual grave-tablets was one of the many innovations that the Romans brought to this country but centuries were to pass before the use of gravestones in churchyards became customary. In fact, when one considers the age of most of our churches and the vast number of burials that must have taken place in the churchyards, one realizes how relatively few gravestones remain. There are many reasons why. We are well aware of the destruction wrought by political and religious factions on both churches and churchyards, but less obviously, the treatment of memorial stones as 'free quarry' accounts for the loss of many gravestones. I have heard a churchwarden say, 'If you need any more stone there are plenty of old gravestones in the churchyard.' Memorials from cleared churchyards are not always disposed of as specified in the faculty – they may be used to pave a parishioner's garden. But surely it is better that they be used thus than as hardcore, for at least they survive with the chance that one

166. Portland, Dorset; St George Reforne. Death in childbirth. Mother and twin daughters who also died shown in tester-bed with guardian angel pulling back drapes, 1775

covered the graves of clerics and priests. The slabs were inscribed with crosses and other symbols of divine office, which is probably why they were taken up and placed within the church. It appears that no attempt was made to preserve the head- and footstones, but a few of these can still be found in our churchyards together with other sepulchral slabs. According to the Rev. Edward L. Cutts there were twenty-one examples in the churchyard at Lympney Stoke, Somerset, in 1849. A visit to the same churchyard in 1968 revealed seventeen examples, eight of which were either completely or partially buried.

The early head- and footstones were small and thick, averaging about 45 cm high and 20 cm thick. These pairs were the same size and shape as each other, and were normally carved identically, the carving usually being some form of cross. Frequently both sides of the stone were carved. At the beginning of the seventeenth century a name was often carved on one of the stones, with the initials and date of death on the other. Sometimes the initials and date sufficed for both head- and footstone, as can be seen at Lower Swell in Gloucestershire.

The late seventeenth and early eighteenth centuries saw a progressive change in the dimensions of both stones – they became taller, wider and thinner while remaining the same as each other both in size and decorative design. The use of the cross as a symbol was abandoned, and only appears in isolated instances until its regrettable and over-enthusiastic revival in the late nineteenth century.

167. Fairford, Gloucestershire; St Mary. Egyptian caryatid, 1823

day they may be 'discovered' and restored? Close inspection of churchyard walls will often reveal fragments of gravestones used in their repair, and they may even, but not surprisingly, appear in the fabric of the church itself. Restoration work carried out in the last century on the church at Bakewell in Derbyshire led to the recovery of a large number of early mediaeval memorials. The possibility of other such discoveries should be borne in mind by those responsible for the demolition of redundant churches. Time has erased the faces from many tombstones, whilst others have simply sunk beneath the level of the ground. The occasional discovery of these is very rewarding, as the earth has both cleaned and preserved them.

In spite of the many hazards that beset churchyard memorials, many early examples do survive. The mediaeval sepulchural slabs or 'coffin-lids' to be seen in many churches mostly originated in the churchyard. There they would have been accompanied by head- and footstones, which marked the extent and orientation of the grave. The slab itself served as a 'body-stone' which protected the place of interment. Those to be seen in churches once

The increase in the size of the stones was simply to facilitate the growing desire to identify the deceased in more detail, and thus emulate the increasing grandeur of the tombs and monuments which were being erected within the church. The headstone was inscribed with the biographical details of the deceased, and the footstone was inscribed with the epitaph. The inscribed surfaces of the stones faced outwards, away from each other and away from the grave space, so that a visitor could read the inscriptions without walking on the grave. It was not until the mid-nineteenth century that the headstone was unaccountably and unreasonably set up to face across the grave.

Many head- and footstones have become separated from each other over the years, and it is often impossible to pair them up again. An instance of an identifiable pair showed that over a period of three hundred years the stones had moved ten metres apart, and in these positions they sank into the ground at the rate of five centimetres in seventeen years.

The epitaphs to be found on footstones range from the laconic to the verbose. At Slaugham in Sussex, a 1745 inscription reads:

'Muze not on
Me for as I
Am so must
You be'

In contrast, at West Hoathly in the same county, one finds an epitaph written in 1753:

'Remember Death and that thou must
E're long be turned into Dust.
Where thou shall Sleep thy Time away
Untill ye last great Judgement Day.
When thou shall rise again and give
Account to God how thou didst live.
For God shall bring
every work into Judgement
with every secret thing whe
ther it be good or whether it be
EVIL.'

The eighteenth century saw the true blossoming of the headstone. As it grew larger and increasingly beautiful, it became customary to cut the epitaph underneath the inscription on the headstone. A large footstone was no longer required so it returned to its original size bearing once more the initials of the deceased and date of death.

The increase in the size of the headstone demanded greater inventiveness from the stonemason, and it is in the eighteenth century that we find the masters of the craft whose skilled carving and letter cutting rivalled, and often

168. Portland, Dorset; St George Reforne. Mourner with willow and urn, 1853

169. Broadway, Worcestershire; St Eadburga. Man supplicant to Death, 1685

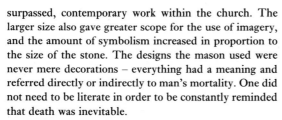

170. Lydney, Gloucestershire; St Mary. Winged head symbol of the soul

171. Bretforton, Worcestershire; St Leonard. Detail of resurrection scene showing archangel, 1797

surpassed, contemporary work within the church. The larger size also gave greater scope for the use of imagery, and the amount of symbolism increased in proportion to the size of the stone. The designs the mason used were never mere decorations – everything had a meaning and referred directly or indirectly to man's mortality. One did not need to be literate in order to be constantly reminded that death was inevitable.

A churchyard is a relatively small space to accommodate innumerable burials over the centuries. Few graves were marked and the sexton must have been constantly digging up skulls and bones. The crypts of some churches are packed full of such churchyard gleanings and it is not surprising that the mason often used both skull and bones as a symbol of death. He also borrowed the pick and spade of the sexton for the same purpose. The hourglass, frequently winged, reminded observers how swiftly time flies, and 'God's Book' in which is written every deed whether it be good or bad, was a very positive way of saying 'Repent, before it is too late!'

Other symbols chosen to represent death were a broken flower or tree (later a broken column), and a shattered hourglass. Death personified took skeletal shape and brandished his dart at his helpless victim. At Broadway in Worcestershire a man kneels pleading with relentless

Death, who is shown driving a dart into the man's heart (1685). At Cocking in Sussex a young girl wearing a contemporary hooped dress leans innocently on a pillar, unaware of the figure of Death standing behind her, dart in hand. Innocent she must have been, as on the other side of the pillar she is shown again, still wearing the same dress but now transformed into an angel by the simple addition of wings (*c.* 1770). Death also came in the more benevolent form of Father Time. He is often shown holding an hourglass in one hand, whilst in the other he holds a scythe with which he effortlessly cuts down a tree.

The mason sometimes turned his thoughts to pleasanter realms, to life after death and that mysterious thing, the soul. The soul is particularly difficult to symbolize having no known form, and the mason, knowing that the soul did not have a body, compromised and showed it as a bodiless head with wings. These winged heads, carved by hundreds of different masons, show vividly the inspiration of the individual. Elegant and rustic, bucolic and divine, they abound in such variety that they would make a study in themselves.

Still very much concerned with the need to save souls, the mason carved scenes showing the end of the world and the general resurrection. Beneath a fanfare of trumpets, buildings are shown falling down, while graves open and

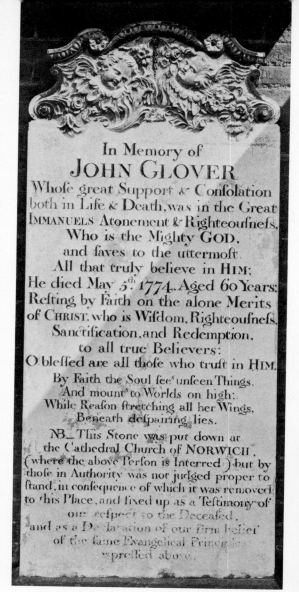

In Memory of
JOHN GLOVER
Whose great Support & Consolation
both in Life & Death, was in the Great
IMMANUELS Atonement & Righteousness,
Who is the Mighty GOD,
and saves to the uttermost,
All that truly believe in HIM;
He died May 5ᵗʰ 1774. Aged 60 Years:
Resting by Faith on the alone Merits
of CHRIST, who is Wisdom, Righteousness,
Sanctification, and Redemption,
to all true Believers:
O blessed are all those who trust in HIM.
By Faith the Soul see unseen Things,
And mount to Worlds on high:
While Reason stretching all her Wings,
Beneath despairing lies.
NB. This Stone was put down at
the Cathedral Church of NORWICH,
(where the above Person is Interred) but by
those in Authority was not judged proper to
stand, in consequence of which it was removed
to this Place, and fixed up as a Testimony of
our respect to the Deceased,
and as a Declaration of our firm belief
of the same Evangelical Principles
expressed above.

172. Mattishall, Norfolk; All Saints. A monument recording its own removal from Norwich Cathedral

their occupants cast off their shrouds and climb out. Various texts (sometimes several on one headstone) were often added to the design to give its meaning emphasis.

The mason was naturally influenced by the architectural innovations with which he became familiar in the normal course of his work and we see this influence reflected in the designs on the gravestones. Rather belatedly he adopted the urn as a symbol of death – inappropriate perhaps when commemorating an interment but surely more at home on a gravestone than on a fireplace.

Some of the most interesting carvings are those that portray a brief moment in the life of the person

commemorated – the scholar with his books; a farmer feeding his geese; a knife-grinder sharpening knives watched by his wife who suckles their child. Accidental death inspired other scenes and one finds falling trees, over-turned wagons and sinking ships, to name but a few examples. One of the most tragic can be seen at Warblington in Hampshire where there is a reminder that press-gangs roamed the streets, forcing young men to fight in the war. Such a young man was William Bean who died in 1758 aged twenty. His headstone is carved showing a ship on fire, while a long boat is rowed away by members of the crew. The inscription tells us that William lost his life when gunpowder caught fire in 'His Majesties Ship

173. Windlesham, Surrey; St John the Baptist. Tombs designed by Sir Edwin Lutyens

The Torbay' in Portsmouth Harbour. The epitaph relates the whole tragic story:

'Unhappy late imprest and forc'd was I
From every Friend, to fight the Enemy.
Yet harder fate by Strange Explosion sent.
From fire to water mark the dire event.
Two Elements conspire to set me free.
Lord from life's tempest rests my soul with thee.'

The tools of a man's trade and the coat of arms of the livery company of his trade suggested more ideas for commemoration, and they provide us with historic evidence of tools and instruments that are no longer used.

Although the masons used the same form of symbolism, they each developed their own particular style. It is this fact which makes our gravestones so fascinating. Stone, too, varies throughout the country, and each type of stone demands a different method of carving, adding further interest.

The lettering on seventeenth-century memorials was very plain and simple, but in the eighteenth century the masons became fascinated with calligraphy and emulated the writing masters of that period. Some were purists and copied the forms devised by the writing masters exactly,

175. March, Cambridgeshire; St Wendreda. Before the grave-yard had been tidied

176. March, Cambridgeshire; St Wendreda. After the graveyard had been tidied

174. Burstow, Surrey; St Bartholomew. Headboards or wooden leaping boards

but others used their own free interpretation of the letter forms. In a churchyard where it is possible to identify a group of stones carved by one mason, one can see how he experimented with letters and designed his own shapes and flourishes.

Looking at the richly ornate gravestones of the period, it is difficult to define how the mason priced his work. One concludes that they were commissioned like works of art, and that the mason put all his artistic skill into creating a thing of beauty. Today, masons are more concerned with profit, and do only the work they are paid for.

The art of the gravestone cutter continued until the middle of the eighteenth century. Over the years he adopted new ideas. Never content to repeat the same idea, he copied the lettering of printers and signwriters and when mourning became fashionable he carved graceful women in widows' weeds, leaning elegantly against pillars and urns, or draping themselves over graves and tombs.

The middle years of the eighteenth century saw changes in the churchyard. Many were closed to further burial because they had become overcrowded and cemeteries were opened to take their place. Marble was imported at competitive prices and this material, which for so long had been the prerogative of the rich, was now available to all. The clergy decided that the symbolism on gravestones was unsuitable for a Christian, condemning absolutely all the forms that this had taken and stating categorically that the only 'fit emblem for a Christian's grave – is the CROSS: that emblem, (alas that I should say it,) is almost never to be seen on our monuments, or in our Church-yards.' The masons, who had shown themselves to be such free-thinkers, followed this rather unfortunate injunction almost to the letter. The spirit went out of their work, and it never recovered.

Someone invented the kerb and the footstone virtually went out of use. The kerb was quite a reasonable innovation – it effectively marked the extent of the grave and protected it from being walked on. But visually it was a disaster.

I have concentrated on head- and footstones, the memorials of the less wealthy parishioners, because they far outnumber all the other tombs to be found in our churchyards. There are of course, many other types of tomb: ornate and elegant box-tombs and chest-tombs; coped-stones and ledgers; table-tombs and pedestal-tombs. Tombs in the shape of sarcophagi, coffins, and pyramids. But whatever form they took, they all served the same purpose – to mark and protect the grave.

Stone was not the only material used. Wood was probably used quite frequently either in the form of a

177. Sandon, Staffordshire; All Saints. An excellent example of the country churchyard, with rough sward providing shelter for wild life

headboard (i.e. taking the shape and the place of the headstone), or as a grave-rail extending over the length of the grave. The inscription was normally painted on. Brick was used, quite effectively, for box-tombs but those that were rendered to look like stone have decayed badly. Head- and footstones, ledgers, box-tombs and grave-rails were copied in cast iron, and artificial stones and even pottery were sometimes used.

The wholesale clearance of churchyards in the pursuit of tidiness started in the eighteenth century and reached fever pitch in the 1950s and '6os. It became fashionable to have a tidy well-kept churchyard which could be entered in 'best kept village' competitions. Bulldozers tore up and shattered memorials, the ground was levelled and grassed and churchyards degenerated into suburban lawns.

This desire for tidiness is still with us but fortunately the economic situation has slowed it down. Perhaps reason will prevail before finances improve, for what is a churchyard other than a place of burial? A place where one can remember the dead, as recommended by Gregory the Great. A place, too, where one becomes aware of oneself as part of a continuing community. A church, standing in a sea of green, deprived of its monuments to past parishioners, loses scale and becomes disorientated, and we become a little disorientated too.

I have allowed very little space for the description of individual monuments. Their diversity is such that no book, however vast, could properly do them justice. However, it is my hope that you will look at churchyards with new interest and understanding and discover for yourselves gravestones of greater interest that any that I could hope to describe.

LITURGY
by Thomas Cocke

Quod semper, quod omnibus, quod ubique. This Latin tag, generally used to define the Catholic doctrine of the Church, can equally apply to most people's conception of the arrangement of a church building. It should have a chancel, nave and aisles, with stalls for the clergy and the choir in the former, and, in the latter, serried pews facing east. The font is at the west end, the pulpit to the north of the chancel arch and the brass eagle lectern to the south, while at the far east end, raised on several steps and surrounded by encaustic tiles, stands the altar with cross and candlesticks. This is the pattern of the Anglican church accepted 'always, by everyone, everywhere'. Yet a hundred years ago many of these elements, such as a surpliced choir in the sanctuary, a cross on the altar or a brass lectern, would have been considered new-fangled if not dangerously Romish; a hundred and fifty years ago the whole arrangement would seem incomprehensible. Thus in seeking new modes of setting our worship, we need not be bound by what are only nineteenth-century versions of our mediaeval heritage; rather, we should look back to the formative and classic centuries of Anglican life, from the Reformation to the Oxford Movement.

For these three hundred years there were two principal ways of ordering churches. One was to 'compartmentalize' the building into separate rooms with distinct functions; the other was to unify it into one hall or 'auditory'. The first system was evolved in the early years of the Reformation as an attempt to adapt mediaeval structures to Protestant worship. The choir or chancel was no longer needed to house large numbers of priests, except in cathedrals. Furthermore, if the minister conducted services from it, as the 1549 Prayer Book directed, he was not only inaudible but he was also setting himself up as an intermediary between God's presence in the sanctuary and the congregation in the nave. The solution eventually enshrined in the Elizabethan Settlement was not to seal off the chancel as extremist reformers like Hooper had desired, but to use it as a special room for the services which required the congregation to approach the altar, above all for the Eucharist but also for marriage and the churching of women. In the Communion, the invitation to 'draw near with faith' was literally obeyed; communicants went up through the screen at the Offertory and remained in the choir until the service ended. The custom largely died out during the eighteenth century but it had already ensured the preservation of much of the Church's mediaeval legacy. The screen between chancel and nave was preserved by a royal order of 1561, losing only its rood loft with the figures of Christ crucified, the Virgin and St John. The chancel itself was not left to fall into decay or to be used as a burial place, as in many Scottish parishes; it was still an integral part of the building even if not in such regular use as the nave. In ex-monastic or collegiate churches the stalls no longer needed by canons could be used by the communicants at the Eucharist. At Cartmel Priory both screen and stalls were restored and embellished in the early seventeenth century.

The nave was regarded as pre-eminently the place for preaching and for Morning and Evening Prayer. The pulpit was thus an essential part of its furniture, to be balanced by a 'decent and convenient' seat for the officiating priest, which became known as the reading desk. George Herbert had them set up in his church of Leighton Bromswold like twin early Christian ambos on either side of the chancel arch, to symbolize that neither should 'have a precedency or priority of the other; but that prayer and preaching, being equally useful, might agree like brethren'.

The idea of separating the church into different rooms could be extended. In 1755 the north transept of St Mary

Redcliffe was made into a special place for baptism with a new carved font, mahogany rails and a marble pavement. The idea could also be applied negatively. It was easy to seal off a useless Lady Chapel and, as at Long Melford, make it into a schoolroom, or, as at Selby Abbey, to allow the nave to be used for a warehouse of market stalls.

The auditory church entered the Anglican tradition in the seventeenth century. It represented a more radical and logical response to the demands of the reformed liturgy. First Inigo Jones' St Paul's, Covent Garden and then Wren's City churches, show an abandonment of the mediaeval forms of structurally distinct chancel, nave and aisles in favour of one great hall with, at most, a shallow recess or apse for the altar. The best summary of their particular suitability for Prayer Book worship was given by Sir Christopher Wren in connection with the Fifty New Churches Act of Queen Anne's reign. He stressed that, unlike Roman Catholics who only need to 'hear the murmur of the Mass and see the Elevation of the Host', Anglican worshippers must be able to follow the officiating clergy with both eye and ear. Churches must therefore be comparatively small and, if necessary, have galleries to bring as many people as possible within range of the minister. Wren recommended his own St James's, Piccadilly as a model; its rectangular plan with galleries on

three sides and the altar on the fourth, holding a congregation of 2000, was 'beautiful and convenient and as such, the cheapest of any Form I could invent'.

Common to both compartmentalized and auditory types of church was a further principle in arrangement, that of multiple focus. The typical Roman church of the period, whether as large as the Gesù or as small as S. Andrea al Quirinale, was centred on the high altar and the sacrament exposed thereon. Side-altars only served to build up to the climax of the east end; pulpits and stalls were only incidents. In the Church of England the place of the altar was, of course, a matter of great controversy for the first century or so after the Reformation. Should it be treated like the mediaeval stone altars and ranged in honour at the east end or like a table be placed lengthwise down the chancel to serve as God's board? Archbishop Laud sought to stress its importance. It was the place where Christ's body was made manifest; in the pulpit Christ's word alone was set forth. Congregations resisted Laud's attempts to force 'the beauty of holiness' on them but, after the violent upheavals of the Civil Wars and the Interregnum, they grew to accept decoration in the sanctuary. By 1700 it was a poor parish that did not have carved and painted tables of the Ten Commandments, the Creed and the Paternoster, hanging above the altar, flanking pictures of Moses and

178. Stanstead Abbots, Hertfordshire; St Andrew. Interior has survived in pre-'ecclesiological' state, remarkably akin to the watercolour of St Paul, Clapham

179. Clapham, South London; St Paul. Interior before nineteenth-century enlargement, showing box-pews and series of superb monuments and hatchments

180. Lyddington, Rutland; St Andrew. Rare seventeenth-century arrangement of sanctuary with Communion rails surrounding Communion table on all four sides

Aaron and, possibly, a gilded 'glory' above, with the divine name inscribed in a triangle. Well-wrought rails protected the sanctuary.

The altar was not, however, exalted above the other liturgical centres, such as the font, the pulpit and the reading desk. The font remained, despite Puritan pressure, in its ancient place at the west end, symbolizing man's entry into the Church by baptism. By the eighteenth century pulpit and reading desk were frequently combined into great 'two deckers', or even 'three deckers' when the lowest tier was formed by the clerk's pew, whence the parish clerk led the congregation's responses and singing. These structures, whether soberly architectural or, like Keene's pulpit for Westminster Abbey now in Trottiscliffe, Kent, gaily Rococo with a palm tree to bear the sounding board, were designed to rise above the high pews then essential against the cold and the draughts of unheated churches. Just as the period's

182. Bristol; Wesley's New Room, Horsfair. Dating from 1739, enlarged in 1748, the first of all Methodist churches

183. Travellers' Rest, Devon. A simple straightforward building, now redundant and in process of conversion to domestic use, with rich late Victorian furnishings

Sunday service moved majestically from Morning Prayer to Litany to Ante or full Communion without dramatic contrasts, so the congregation's attention could be fixed on whatever was the chief area of interest for the particular service. No irreverence was meant if to look at the pulpit involved turning away from the altar.

Artistically the consequence was that the various fittings have a unity and uniformity of standard rather than a dramatic development. A high standard in the execution of pedimented reredos or black and white marble floor was more prized than iconographical innovation.

The Tractarians despised this utilitarian attitude which by the era of the Waterloo churches had, indeed, sunk to a concern for economy and convenience regardless of beauty or tradition. They returned the priest to the sanctuary and further isolated him by interposing a cathedral-style choir between him and the congregation. The altar, raised up and 'restored' free of intervening screens and tympana, however ancient, was now the focus of the building. Thus was created the High Victorian church, which, civilized and Catholicized towards the turn of the century by the suave mediaevalism of Bodley and the Alcuin Club, became the classic Anglican interior.

What value today has this rapidly sketched story, well enough known to scholars if not to the 'man in the pew'? Firstly, it may enrich understanding of England's own ecclesiastical inheritance and, hopefully, encourage efforts already made to find ideas for modern worship in ancient precedent. A nave altar need not mean the abandonment of the chancel but its transformation into a specialized room for particular services; a surpliced choir seated in the sanctuary need not be the *sine qua non* of a respectable church; instrumental ensembles can replace organs. Secondly, an appreciation of the variety of the past will lead to a more balanced judgement of its legacy of church fittings. A Georgian interior has value in its completeness and consistency, not just as an assemblage of well-carpentered furniture to be moved or altered at will; conversely, Victorian fittings, be they screens, lamps or even, in certain cathedrals, stoves, have positive aesthetic and historic interest. They should not be discarded wholesale in an attempt to escape from nineteenth-century ideas of worship. *Stare super antiquas vias*, that good Anglican vice, involves not dull persistence in the ways of the recent past but stimulating adventures into the diversities of many centuries.

181. East Heslerton, Yorkshire; St Andrew. By George Edmund Street, 1877, one of a series of churches built or restored for an enlightened patron, Sir Tatton Sykes. Furnishings all by Street and chancel vaulted in stone

ARCHAEOLOGY
by Richard Morris

As I can scan my bookcase I see volumes and papers dealing with a wide variety of ecclesiological topics: fonts, screens, monuments, bells, churchyards, heraldry, mouldings, towers, plate, sculpture, glass, materials, roofs, carpentry, wallpaintings, dedications. Strangely, few authors have attempted to combine these various strands of study, even in a general way. A comparable division exists in the field of historical research (on a lower shelf) wherein the history of the Church and the history of churches have virtually become separate issues of scholarship. That architectural studies, too, are becoming increasingly specialized is reflected in the growth of organizations which owe their existence to interest in or concern for buildings belonging to a particular phase of architectural history. Bodies such as the Georgian and Victorian Societies, for example, deal with churches only insofar as they fall within certain historical or stylistic limits. The value of such bodies is of course beyond question, but care is wanted if we are not to slip into an attitude of mind which regards history as a series of well-defined episodes, complete and satisfying in themselves, rather than as a continuum; a continuum, moreover, which is nowhere better illustrated than in the growth of a parish and its church. In saying this it is necessary to remember that a church as it is *now* may only be the most recent structure in a sequence. Although the church is commonly the oldest building surviving in a village, successive additions and rebuildings will often have blurred or obliterated signs of the early history of the site and structure. Many a Scott or a Street stands guard over an Anglo-Saxon predecessor.

Probably the most alarming aspect of the tendency to split rather than to combine church studies is the way in which modern methods of caring for churches have become divorced from the processes of investigating and understanding them. Architects are no longer expected to interpret or record mediaeval churches in their care, merely to repair them. Many operations which nowadays are thought essential to preserve the appearance of churches or to keep them in good structural order are harmful to what might be described as the latent history of ecclesiastical buildings. Some simple examples will illustrate the point: the digging of a trench around the base of a church to combat rising damp may destroy the remains of an Anglo-Saxon *porticus*; rewiring may involve the chiselling of conduit channels through plaster which, although blank on the surface, may contain inner laminations bearing mediaeval decoration; in the tower, the re-hanging of bells may lead to the removal without record of an ancient bell-frame which itself may have been put together with pieces of timber obtained from an earlier roof. We may like to think that such incidents are exceptional, but the truth is that they are far more common than we suspect. Projects of restoration and repair, being intended to maintain or enhance the outward, surface appearance of churches, can seriously affect the hidden history of ecclesiastical buildings.

The conflict between history and maintenance is no fault of architects, or of the diocesan committees whose task it is to monitor and regulate repairs and changes in churches. Indeed, many of these committees have practising archaeologists among their members. The root of the problem lies in the trend to which I drew attention at the outset: the growing preoccupation with externals, detail and parts, and the breakdown of communication which inevitably arises when what is essentially a single subject-area becomes splintered into disjointed specializations. The problem has been intensified, however, because archaeological interest in the historical potential of churches has been reawakened at a time when the

184. York; St Helen on the Walls. Excavation revealed a small Anglo-Scandinavian church, sited over Roman mosaics, to which additions and rebuilds were made prior to demolition in the sixteenth century

parochial structure and the deployment of the Church's resources are coming under close and sometimes critical scrutiny. The task of those who believe in the need to preserve, record or investigate the evidence which is latent within and around our churches can become complicated by those who see churches solely in relation to present and future needs and would minimize the value of any enhanced consciousness of the past. I know of at least one mediaeval church which is likely to be demolished in the near future for no better reason than that its redundancy is thought to be a bad advertisement for the state of the Faith. In certain areas this is a point of view which might be justified, but this particular church has been empty since the village which it served was deserted in the thirteenth century.

The tension between history and pastoral needs is a subject to which I shall return at the end of this article, but first it is necessary to develop two themes from my opening paragraphs: the legacy of historical evidence which is contained within our churches, and the ways in which this legacy is being put at risk.

The traditional place to seek hidden evidence in a church is underneath it. Here footings, a succession of floors, vaults and sometimes the lower courses of walls may be revealed. Often these will indicate that the church has had an architectural history of far greater length and complexity than might be anticipated from an inspection of the upstanding fabric alone. The absence of obvious structural remains is no guarantee that structures did not exist. Building stone has always been at a premium, and materials from old walls and footings were frequently re-used, leaving nothing but the old construction trenches and the backfill with which the structures were replaced. It is possible to reconstruct the plan of a building which has vanished in this way, but it takes an experienced eye and the recording must take place under controlled conditions. Evidence of former timber structures, too, is easily missed. Where a repair or conversion has gone ahead in the absence of an archaeologist the architect or builder will often state reassuringly that 'we took up the floor but there was nothing underneath'.

However, it is essential that we should free ourselves from the popular view of the archaeologist which concentrates on the idea that he is only concerned with what lies beneath the ground. In the case of an historic church the distinction between above- and below-ground evidence is unreal and without relevance. Stratification is a law which applies to structures as well as to the ground in which they are planted. A wall can scarcely be considered apart from the foundation which carries it; it is right to

view an early floor in relation to the roof which sheltered it. The advantage of considering above- and below-ground evidence together lies in the fact that features in one or other artificial category which may be inexplicable when viewed in isolation can slip into focus and become intelligible. Thus a scatter of chippings which might be meaningless if excavated on an open site may be seen to have accumulated during the carving of a capital *in situ*; a post-hole may relate to a stage in the construction of the roof; a pit under the modern floor may have been used to cast the bell which hangs in the tower; mediaeval glazed floor tiles may have been taken up at the Reformation and used to patch a parapet; a Victorian heating engineer may have found some Anglo-Saxon voussoirs to be useful supports for his underfloor piping. The archaeology of a church is something total, concerning the entire fabric and its contents. It is not to be divided.

Such details and glimpses of the past might be thought interesting, but it could fairly be argued that in themselves they form a poor reward for the expense and effort involved in their recovery. At this stage it is necessary to draw back from detail, away from the notion that churches are art-objects or buildings of interest exclusively in themselves, and to take a broader view in which churches can be considered in relation to the communities they serve.

Within the community the church had a special place, which it often retains. Until the Reformation a church was much more than a building. It served as a community centre, stronghold, storehouse, school, and theatre. The porch and graveyard were places of assembly and 'the scene of transactions'. The position of the church and the antiquity of its site may have influenced the development of the village plan. In towns we find the church to be a sensitive indicator of the wealth, enterprise and variety of urban life. The location of a church near the core of a town of Roman origin sometimes gives a clue as to the extent to which the topography and occasionally the institutions of the Roman town governed developments during the Anglo-Saxon period. From about the tenth century town churches begin to signal markets, quarters specializing in a particular trade or manufacturing process, an ethnic pocket within the larger population, a local cult. The church in the inner suburb marks the point at which the mediaeval town once strayed into the countryside. The parish boundaries of churches in a late Saxon planned town may ignore the regular grid of streets and indicate a pre-urban, rural pattern.

The rural pattern is itself far from being a simple matter of a church in every village. Just when does the nucleated

185. Deerhurst, Gloucestershire; St Mary. Excavation below ground has enlarged the area of wall available for study. This shows the junction of the north porticus with a later north-west porticus below modern ground level. Stones in the left hand foundation are re-used Roman, stones re-used in the right hand foundation include Saxon grave slabs

186. Deerhurst, Gloucestershire; St Mary. The east wall of the north porticus (later north aisle) showing the original doorway for the north-east porticus with herringbone walling at low level. The porticus was later raised in height; and aumbries were cut into the wall in the fourteenth century and the door blocked when this aisle was used as the Cassye family chapel. The wall has been stripped of mid-nineteenth-century plaster to permit structural analysis and recording

village become the normal unit of lowland settlement in England, and how many eccentrically sited churches afford a glimpse of some previous pattern of dispersed settlement? How do we explain the striking correspondence between certain ecclesiastical parishes and earlier secular boundaries, some of which at least can be traced back to Romano-British estates? Were church sites ever selected because of their pagan associations? What were the origins of churchyard burial? The fact that many of these themes must be expressed as questions is an illustration of the extent to which we are underinformed about our churches. The belief that churches form a well-studied class of monument is a fallacy; for the most part study has been restricted to architectural detail, or to specific aspects of church history approached in isolation.

Returning to the church building itself for a moment, the fabric and the archaeological evidence which it may contain can assist us in penetrating the nature of mediaeval belief. Accustomed as we are to a desymbolized world of Protestant values it is hard to visualize the role of the Roman Catholic Church and the appearance of its churches prior to the awakening reason and the icon-

oclasm of the Reformation. The ritual, imagery, cults, superstitions and recurring cycle of the Church calendar were embodied and externalized in the plan, internal arrangements and decoration of the mediaeval parish church. Form is an expression of function, and the architectural setting for worship is the mirror in which liturgical ceremonies and mediaeval ideas can be recognized.

It would be a mistake, however, to view mediaeval churches entirely in terms of the piety of their founders. As much as anything churches represent wealth: endowments, gifts, tithes. During the Anglo-Saxon period many churches were founded and endowed as sources of profit. It is no coincidence that churches in the Domesday Book are usually listed along with other items of village revenue-producing plant, such as mills and fishponds. The physical development of a church building will often be an index to the history of the community it serves. Prosperity may have prompted the addition of an aisle or tower. An economic boom may have led to the complete rebuilding of a church, and a consequent obliteration of all the stages of growth which may have preceded it. Caution is needed

187. Little Somborne, Hampshire; All Saints. Before restoration. Superficially it looks a very simple building

188. Little Somborne, Hampshire; All Saints. During restoration. When stripped down to a skeleton it becomes something very complicated involving both above and below ground archaeology

in the interpretation of such evidence, however, since the wealth of an individual patron could be sufficient to offset the reality of poverty among the ordinary members of the congregation, or even the complete absence of a congregation. Many a ruined church in Norfolk shows signs of progressive enlargement until the end of the mediaeval period in circumstances where it seems clear that the local population was as sparse then as it is now. On the other hand, the astonishing concentration of churches in East Anglia is surely a sign than the early-mediaeval population in that area was not only much larger than we might imagine but was also grouped in a shifting pattern of

189. Rudston, Yorkshire; All Saints. Pagan monolith with a mediaeval church

190. Castlegate, York; St Mary. Anglo-Scandinavian cross bases made from Roman columns were discovered during the conversion of the church into an architectural heritage centre. Subsequent excavations revealed some of the eleventh-century church

communities which had already undergone considerable alteration before the Conquest.

However, in the absence of a patron, poverty could stunt the growth of a parish church, thereby leaving it unaltered down to our own time. The connection between isolated churches and deserted villages is well known, and hardly needs elaboration here, except to stress that the factors which caused desertion were more varied than is popularly supposed; epidemic was one of the rarer reasons; a shift in the economic balance of a region was the common cause. Recession, or more usually enclosure followed by depopulation, might lead to the contraction of a church which was formerly much larger, or to total abandonment. A blocked arcade, a shortened chancel, an unfinished tower: these may sometimes be the only record of changing fortunes. In mediaeval towns the numbers of churches frequently exceeded pastoral needs. Even before the Reformation many urban churches had already disappeared. In these cases archaeological investigation, while lacking the above-ground structural dimension, may reveal the liturgical layout of a mediaeval church without the overlay and disturbance of subsequent alterations.

Viewed individually churches will narrate the economic and social history of the communities they were built to serve. Considered collectively churches illustrate much larger patterns: of trade, cultural contact, the transport of materials, and the transmission of ideas.

In the foregoing paragraphs I have tried to bring to attention the importance of viewing churches in relation to their surroundings, and to stress the value of an archaeological approach to their study. I do not use the word 'archaeological' in any narrow sense, but rather as an umbrella term which covers a comprehensive process of enquiry in which the skills of the architectural historian, geographer, documentary historian, excavator and architect are brought into alliance. The scope of the study is large. It spans the period between the introduction of Christianity into Britain in the Roman era until the present. The objective is a clearer understanding of the origins and growth of the Church in Britain – its periods of expansion, decay and revival – seen in relation to the social and topographical evolution of our villages, towns and countryside. It is in this context that small items of information obtained by archaeological investigation in individual churches must be considered. The aim is not to amass useless detail, but to grasp the broader picture.

Unfortunately much of the evidence is vulnerable to disturbance during the course of normal care and maintenance. Attention has already been drawn to the archaeologically destructive effects of repair and restoration in historic churches. Restoration is in fact a misleading word; 'reconstitution' would often be more accurate, for we are gradually remaking our mediaeval churches. A new floor, underpinning, repointing or plastic repair may all in their way blot out some aspect of the history of a church and its site. Obviously such operations must take place; what is not always recognized, however, is that they may offer the only opportunity to record archaeological evidence which thereafter has to be destroyed. The situation is all the more urgent because the number of churches in use is now falling. We cannot replenish our mediaeval heritage – it is a wasting asset – but we surely have a duty to record it as and when it becomes necessary to repair, convert, demolish, re-order or abandon churches. Considered in total, single episodes of archaeological destruction add up to major loss.

These may seem to be discouraging words, of little practical comfort to the struggling parish already faced with rising costs and exhausted by endless fund raising. Reroofing the nave and curing the damp in the chancel is expensive enough ... but to pay for archaeological research at the same time? I see the problem, but I also believe that the history of a church should form part of the responsibility of those who use it. Part of the difficulty may lie in the public attitude to archaeology. Often it is assumed that the archaeologist is motivated only by personal curiosity; the 'right' to investigate is extended as a kind of privilege (to be withdrawn if it looks like becoming inconvenient); and the results of the investigation are thought of as in some way 'belonging to' the archaeologist, and as having no wider significance. In fact the archaeologist is simply a servant. He translates information from a physical to a written medium. Dr Bernard Feilden summed up the matter exactly when he wrote: 'If we attach value to knowledge, and thereby would be civilized, then the motivation for the gathering of knowledge must come from us as a community – even though we may delegate the work. The community should have the right to enjoy the fruits of the research, but if it does then it also has an obligation to provide the means.'

The fundamental question, then, is not 'who pays?' but 'who is ultimately *responsible* for the protection or recording of the history in and around this church?' If parishes shoulder this responsibility they will find that there are others to whom they can delegate the task of raising money and carrying out the work. But to avoid the responsibility is also to avoid the truth, and to willingly enter a kind of darkness.

ASPECTS OF CRAFTSMANSHIP

191. Charlwood, Surrey; St Nicholas. Wallpaintings depicting St Margaret (*c.* 1350), and the Three Dead (late fourteenth century); rediscovered in the nineteenth century

192. Sandon, Staffordshire; All Saints. Group of monuments to members of the Erdeswick family with extremely rare *trompe l'oeil* painting of Y-traceried window and family tree of Samson Erdeswick, d. 1603, whose monument is on the left

194. Ingestre, Staffordshire; St Mary. Probably by Sir Christopher Wren, 1676, with plasterwork of high quality comparable to Wren's city churches

193. Torquay, Devon; St Luke. High Victorian decorative scheme on chancel walls and roof, recently revived

195. Hampnett, Gloucestershire. Norman chancel and chancel arch with decorative scheme revived during the nineteenth century – probably following traces of the original

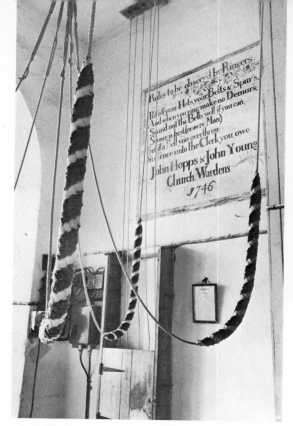

196. Lydlinch, Dorset; St Thomas Becket. An uncommon example of a rustic text with a monition to the bellringers, painted directly on to the wall

197. Lea, Wiltshire; St Giles. Bell of 1622, with Prince of Wales feathers

198. Hardington Somerset; St Mary. Hatchment, painted on canvas; carried in the funeral procession of the nobility and gentry these were then hung in the parish church and many survive

199. Stanton Fitzwarren. Wiltshire; St Leonard. A circular Norman font with carving of exceptional quality depicting the eight Virtues and Vices

200. Trent, Dorset; St Andrew. Fourteenth-century bell, with a fine early twentieth-century stock bearing the name of the bell founders.

PART TWO
POINTS OF VIEW

DIOCESAN ADVISORY
COMMITTEES
by The Very Revd Tony Bridge

Since the time of the Reformation, the incumbent of a parochial benefice in the Church of England has been protected from interference by bishops (and, indeed, by anyone else) by security of tenure and a legally guaranteed freedom of action which few other people have ever enjoyed. This has had mixed results; idle parsons have been in no danger of eviction; theological free thinkers have freely thought, sometimes but by no means always to the great benefit of the Church; country clergy have indulged passions for lepidoptery, palaeontology, or whatever; extreme eccentrics have enriched the English social scene in a variety of highly improbable ways; and until this century the clergy have often treated their churches, *de facto* if not strictly *de jure*, as places which were as much theirs to do with as they liked as their vicarages or even their potting sheds. This was the kind of thing lampooned by Sir John Betjeman in his early poem, which begins 'The Church's restoration in eighteen-eighty-three,' and ends, referring to the rector, 'Look up! and oh how glorious, he has restored the roof!' Churchwardens were often as bad as parsons at doing more or less what they pleased to their churches, and rich parishioners seldom found it difficult to get permission to erect the most splendid – and sometimes the most splendidly inappropriate – monuments to themselves or to members of their family in their own parish churches. Bishops were seldom consulted and rarely interfered.

Legally, however, they had the right to do so. At the time of the Reformation a Court of Faculties was set up by the Archbishop of Canterbury to grant on his behalf the various dispensations, licences, and faculties which had hitherto been granted by the Pope, and any alteration to a church building could only be legally made when such a faculty had been obtained. After the First World War it was determined that this law, observed for so long more often in the breach than in any other way, should be strictly enforced. At this time churches throughout the country were threatened with a flood of public and private memorials to men killed between 1914 and 1918, and many of them were artistically deplorable. There is nothing like bereavement to bring out the vulgarian and the sentimentalist in all of us, as a visit to almost any English, Italian, French, or German cemetery will show, and as a nodding acquaintance with the Forest Lawns in California proves beyond doubt. Moreover, with the

coming of imported foreign marble, mirror-polished granite, cheap and ugly stained glass (usually manufactured by commercial firms with little artistic interest and less ability), and the whole ghastly range of mass-produced church furnishings, the time had come to call a halt and revive the old law. Plainly, the Dean of the Arches presiding over the Archbishop's Court of Faculties could not be expected to cope with every request for a faculty, but fortunately there was provision for a consistory court in each diocese, and these courts could easily deal with all requests for faculties within their own diocesan boundaries. The chancellor of each diocese, appointed by the bishop, was the judge in these consistory courts, and it was agreed that in future nothing should be changed in a church building without a faculty from the diocesan chancellor. But since it could not safely be assumed that each chancellor would possess the combined virtues of Ruskin, Roger Fry and Lord Clark, it was decided that some of them would need advice on aesthetic matters, and in 1923 the bishop of each diocese was required to appoint a committee of men qualified to offer such advice. Thus were born the Diocesan Advisory Committees.

Their membership varies from diocese to diocese, but archdeacons are *ex officio* members, while the remainder are appointed by the bishop. Architects are usually present in some numbers, and a great deal of the hard work of going to look at a particular church where some alteration or other is proposed falls on their shoulders; people with a special love and knowledge of old churches are also nearly always invited to serve; and specialists in their own fields make up the rest of the membership. These may include people with expert knowledge of such subjects as campanology, church organs, stained glass, metalwork, archives, libraries, muniments, sculpture, mediaeval mural painting, and so on. Finally, it is becoming more and more usual to appoint an archaeologist to the Committee.

The job of a Diocesan Advisory Committee is purely advisory. Every proposed alteration to a church building, to its graveyard, or to its furniture must be submitted to the Committee which then advises the chancellor either to grant or to withold a faculty for the necessary work; but the chancellor is free to reject the Committee's advice on pastoral or other grounds if he so decides. He does not often do so, and when he does, usually he has good reason; though (in my opinion) there have been a few instances of chancellors abusing their freedom to ignore the advice tendered to them, and there will probably be a few more in the future. Chancellors are not infallible, and some are less so than others. In fairness it should also be said, however, that the advice given by a Diocesan Advisory Committee may on occasions be pernickety, over-scrupulous, and pedantic. This is in part a result of the tedium of much of the work the Committee has to do; judging the aesthetic merits, for example, of a small stained glass window a couple of feet high to be placed under a gallery in a red-brick church built in 1920 is not an inspiring way of spending a morning. On the other hand, some of the work is both exciting and extremely difficult. For example, should a handful of parochial church-goers responsible for an architecturally beautiful church which is badly in need of structural repairs costing a very large amount of money be allowed to sell one of their treasures – a pair of seventeenth-century silver flagons, perhaps, which are never used – in order to help pay for the necessary work? Or, to take another hypothetical example, should an ornate Victorian screen, erected in an Early English church in 1880, be removed, thus restoring the church to its original condition, despite the fact that the screen is an admirable one of its kind and time? Such problems come before the Committee regularly, and they are never easily resolved.

But on the whole, even though both chancellors and their advisers may make mistakes from time to time, the system works tolerably well, and our churches are protected nowadays from the well-meaning but all too often hopelessly misguided attentions of those who wish to 'improve' them in various catastrophic ways, and who have in the past been free to do so.

DISPOSABLE TREASURES
by the Very Revd R. S. Wingfield-Digby

The sale of treasures from parish churches is the subject of continuing debate. The situation has been aggravated by inflation, the escalating cost of stipends for the clergy and the cost of repairs to the fabric of church buildings. Advocates of the sale of church treasures question the value of having gold and silver plate stored away in bank vaults, when it could be sold in the open market for substantial amounts of cash which could be used for major emergency fabric repairs, or be given away to relieve poverty and starvation in other parts of the world.

Ancient parish churches have acquired a variety of treasures through the generosity of worshippers and well-wishers, and the desire to remember the departed. For many centuries before museums came into existence, they were repositories for objects of artistic and historic value: monuments, incunabula and vessels of many shapes and sizes including sacred vessels set apart for eucharistic use

such as chalices, patens, flagons and cruets. The early Christian chalices were commonly made of glass, but the use of any material other than metal was forbidden by the ninth century. After the Reformation a return was made to the former practice of administering communion in both the consecrated bread and wine, which meant that larger chalices had to be made. Over 3000 of these Elizabethan communion cups are known to be in existence.

Faculty jurisdiction controls the disposal of treasures from parish churches in the Church of England, but it may be noted that the number of faculties granted for the sale of historic silver has been declining during the present decade. In the six years from 1970 to 1975 diocesan chancellors granted 11, 6, 5, 5, 3, 2 petitions respectively for the sale of historic plate, and it would appear that they did so reluctantly. The Historic Churches Preservation Trust has also discouraged churches from selling their treasures by refusing repair grants to parishes where such sales have taken place.

The Church of England Council for Places of Worship, a permanent council of the General Synod, set up a working party to study the problem of the Church's inherited treasures. In its 1973 interim report, entitled *Treasures on Earth*, the working party, whose chairman is the Dean of Guildford, recommended that there should be a ten year gap between treasures being in use in parish churches and their sale by parishes wishing to divest themselves of unwanted valuables, and that only one third of the proceeds of sale should belong of right to the parish concerned, the remainder being administered by the Diocesan Board of Finance in favour of any church in the diocese in need of assistance with repair of its fabric. After debating this issue the Synod asked the working party to think again and come back with a modified and more generally acceptable alternative plan.

The other recommendation of the working party relating to the insurance of ecclesiastical treasures was commended by General Synod to all dioceses. Valuables in use in churches need be insured only for the price of a good modern replacement. Widespread acceptance of this advice could have the effect of bringing back into use sacred vessels that have been hidden away in bank vaults for many years.

Risk of theft of valuables in the custody of incumbents and churchwardens is frequently given as a reason for selling them. A modern bronze ewer fashioned by Leslie Durbin was stolen from a parish church and found a few months later in use as a flower vase, in the front parlour of a house in the same town, although the donor's inscription was clearly marked upon it. After it had been returned to the font it was stolen again and not rediscovered. Simple security measures such as a chain and padlock or removal to a locked vestry when not in use would be a way of obviating such a misfortune.

It is not easy to legislate for the sale of treasures. Each case needs consideration on its merits. Vessels that have been set apart for sacred use have acquired a spiritual value, even a special sanctity, which makes them unsuitable for sale in the open market. Some have inscriptions indicating that they were given for use in Holy Communion 'for ever'. Typical inscriptions read 'Dedicated to the service of God'. One such gift from the rector of a parish has inscribed underneath 'The Sacramental Cup is consigned with pious reverence to the Service of the Altar for ever as a testimony of his regard to the parish with the sincere hope that the said element it shall enclose may virtually convey to the humble communicants (may they abound!) from generation to generation, spiritual grace here, the sure pledge of eternal happiness hereafter, 24th June, 1830, the 30th year of his incumbency.' It is arguable that the donor's clearly expressed wishes constitute an obligation to continue the trust, but if the vessel has been stored away for nearly half a century in a bank vault, has not the donor's purpose been frustrated and the trust already been broken?

The Goldsmiths' Company has done much to check dispersal of church plate by generously providing treasuries in cathedrals at Winchester, York, Lincoln, Norwich, Oxford, Chichester and elsewhere, where parish churches can deposit their finest pieces of plate on loan for safe keeping and viewing by the general public. If museum directors are notified immediately a petition for sale in the open market is granted, they will stretch their finances to the limit to buy in treasures of national importance. The Redundant Churches Fund insists that churches handed over to its protection should be complete with all their fittings and treasures wherever possible.

The Church has ever been a patron of the arts. Its treasures have been used to embellish the worship of God and they are part of England's history, part of the national heritage. In my view we should be reluctant to part with them, but keep them in living churches so that generations to come may echo the words of Jacob awaking from his dream 'How awe-inspiring this place is! This is nothing less than a house of God; this is the gate of heaven.'

THE SALE OF TREASURES FROM CATHOLIC CHURCHES
by James Lees-Milne

Throughout the Dark Ages and during the mediaeval and Renaissance periods the Catholic Church was the greatest inspiration of western art, the greatest patron of artists. Churches were built and adorned, firstly, for the glory of God and, secondly, for the worship and delight of the people. These purposes, in this order, persisted throughout Europe and the Christian world until the present century. Holiness and beauty walked hand in hand.

But with decreasing spiritual fervour, artists tended to derive less inspiration from religion. Fewer works of art were dedicated to it. When the clergy wished to embellish their churches they generally found a substitute for art in a kind of whimsy arty-craftiness. Of course there have been exceptional cases of clerical enlightenment. A handful of churches of architectural merit arose in the early decades of this century. In our own country, competent artists like Comper, Gill and Evie Hone were commissioned for ecclesiastical works. In the 1940s Henry Moore executed a statue of Our Lady and Graham Sutherland a painting of the Crucifixion for St Matthew, Northampton. In more recent years Piper and Reyntiens have produced stained glass windows of high quality. But examples of discerning patronage by individual incumbents of churches have become fewer and further between. On the whole church artefacts from 1900 to 1960 were in extremely poor taste. It was a case of the holier the uglier.

Then came the Second Vatican Council of 1962–6, and to everyone's surprise, things suddenly went from bad to worse. The Council brought about a relaxation of the reins of authority. Power passed from the Pope and Curia to the local bishops and priests who adopted a policy of aggressive iconoclasm. The Council had permitted the use of the vernacular in the Roman rite. But the bishops distorted this permission into an obligation. They thus jettisoned the universal Latin liturgy, which had served since the first Christian centuries and was made absolute by Pope Pius V in 1570. They substituted vernacular translations which were often unbelievably commonplace. Furthermore they vetoed or discouraged many of the old Catholic usages and traditions. They frowned upon accessories like holy water and incense, and sacred salutations, like genuflections and the sign of the cross, which had been practised since time immemorial. The bishops then set about despoiling the churches themselves. It may seem an extraordinary state of affairs to exist in an anciently established and divine institution. But this is what happened and is still going on.

Like Cromwell's soldiers, the bishops and clergy turned upon the church treasures. These were not always great works of art, but rather things given by the devout in honour of their dead, or the saints, and gratefully accepted by the clergy of the time. The objects – let us call them *bondieuseries* – contributed to the beauty of the buildings and helped to sustain religious faith. Today the *bondieuseries* – statues, candelabra, chalices, vestments, jewelled reliquaries, votive offerings – are being thrown out, given away, sold. God knows what happens to them in England. In Italy they can be bought in every antique shop and junk market. The parishioners, to whom in a sense these objects belong, are not consulted, nor are they told to what purpose the accruing funds are devoted. The whole business is conducted *sub rosa*, and those people who have the temerity to enquire are either snubbed or ignored. A letter of mine about the sale of church treasures, published in *The Times* on 27 March 1976, elicited no response from the hierarchy.

In France, Italy, and even Spain, where the majority of churches of architectural merit are Catholic – in this country the majority are Anglican and so less likely to be sacked – high altars and side chapels are being ripped to pieces. Ten years ago I saw the Louis XV panelling of the side chapels at Beauvais rotting in the rain outside the cathedral, where it had been dumped. In Italy oratories erected by pious confraternities are closed and the priests forbidden to say Mass in them. In Spain, too, churches are being systematically stripped bare to resemble Nonconformist conventicles.

Priests and officiating clergy are no longer inclined to preach from pulpits or sit in their canopied stalls, presumably because they do not want to appear remote from, or superior to, the congregation. If only they realized that the laity expect and want their pastors to be different from and holier than themselves. The high altar of St James's, Spanish Place, London, has been dismantled. Pugin's rood screen in St Chad's, Birmingham, has been removed. Had it not been accepted by an Anglican parish church it would doubtless now be on a scrap heap. Pugin's high altar in St Augustine's Abbey, Ramsgate, has been given away. The altar rails of St Philip's, Finchley, in which the donor's daughter was recently married, had to the donor's surprise been removed without so much as a by-your-leave. Rare liturgical books belonging to St John's, Norwich, have been sold for no reason that any parishioner can ascertain.

These random examples of seemingly senseless despoliation are among hundreds, if not thousands in England, Wales and Scotland; and literally tens of thousands on the continent.

I have written 'seemingly senseless despoliation'. But how much of this prevailing iconoclasm in the Catholic Church is in fact perpetrated without a purpose? That is the question which requires investigation. But the hierarchy will give no direct explanation. They steadfastly refuse to vouchsafe any reasons that make sense. They may murmur about the spirit of the times being unsuited to splendour and pageantry (*triumphalism* is the pejorative word they bandy) and that it is wrong for churches to contain adornments when there is starvation in the Third World. But the Third World appears to be deriving little benefit from the dispersal from European churches of objects the presence of which helped to draw people to God far more than sermons. After all faith is an emotional, not a cerebral, revelation.

The only conclusion to be drawn from the Catholic Church's *volte-face* from patronage to philistinism is a sinister one. It is political. The Roman Catholic Church today seems more concerned with social egalitarianism than the mysteries of the spirit.

THE CARE OF CHURCHES
by Peter Cleverly

Most people, it would seem, deplore the demise, in name at least, of the former Council for the Care of Churches and, though the Council for Places of Worship may be a more ecumenical body, its title does little to inspire those who operate under its influence. Names are important to define purposes and, when in doubt on any matter of general policy, it is helpful to be able to consider the purpose of any organization which we serve as defined by its title.

In the field of historic buildings (sometimes called ancient monuments) and amongst those bodies which are concerned with their maintenance, the search for an all-embracing name has been continuous. Thus we sometimes speak of repair, of restoration, of preservation, of conservation and protection. All these words have specific meanings.

Repair must mean to mend. It may mean to mend by the most direct and the most economical means but, unless it is considered as an aspect of one or more of the other activities mentioned above, it may not, in itself, be enough. Restoration must presumably mean restoration to the *status quo ante*, but here is a problem for we have to ask ourselves which *status* and *ante* what? Are we to return to our notion of a previous condition? Possibly, but by no means universally, this may be the answer, but such a policy may well conflict with a philosophy of preservation.

The two words 'preservation' and 'conservation' may be considered together and alternatively in the terms of the introduction to the publication of the European Architectural Heritage Year Awards where it was stated, 'to preserve may be taken to mean as far as possible to retain in fact the total integrity of the structure with its original finishes, decorative features, its landscape setting, and so on. To conserve has come to have a wider meaning which can embrace the rational use, re-use, adaptation, extension and enhancement of scarce assets.' Thus preservation denotes preservation of the *status quo* with all its faults and its idiosyncracies, while conservation would seem, in these terms, to mean adaptation to an alternative use. The society from which all that is best in this field has stemmed elected to describe itself as a society for 'Protection'. A hundred years ago protection, while it certainly implied protection from the elements, must also have had the wider meaning of protection from demolition or desecration. Whereas, of course, protection in the narrower sense must still be a perpetual preoccupation, responsibility for protection from destruction has been assumed by central government on a wider scale than could ever be available to any voluntary body however well-disposed and however powerful. Despite many failures and omissions, the Town and Country Acts, various, have done more to resist the pressures of the mid-twentieth century than could the efforts of any combination of voluntary bodies.

In particular relation to churches, all these words have their place and it is possible to imagine a church where the leaded roof covering to the tower has been repaired; the sedilia have been restored; ancient stone has been preserved; the churchyard has been protected (by the frustration of an application to widen the road) and the whole has been conserved by the removal of an enclosing fence and the integration of a churchyard into the communal open space of the neighbourhood.

Such combination of circumstances would, in one word, add up to Care. This excellent word cannot be too often used and it is proper to remind members of DACs that in full they are the Diocesan Advisory Committees for the Care of Churches. Care is continuous. One may restore and go. One may preserve – as a fly in amber – and leave, but if the responsibility to care is undertaken it must be for ever. Continuous care was the traditional mode in which all historic buildings other than churches were once maintained. Some part of the annual income of any estate was devoted to its principal building or buildings. The work of maintenance was – here a little; there a little; line upon line, precept upon precept. Churches have not been so fortunate and have relied on periodic benefactions. It is a common observation that most churches have a considerable face-lift about once every hundred years. Living as we do in 1976, almost exactly a hundred years after the epicentre of a cyclone of activity in restoring churches, it is frequently said that major restoration is now required on almost every ancient church in the country. Many regard the continuation to its logical extreme of this sentiment with dread. Many feel that large capital sums or the fruit of large appeals are not the proper way to deal with historic buildings if their textural quality is to be maintained. Yet the idea of large capital grants designed, as it were, to lock the structure up for another hundred years, is almost universal. This, which seems mild enough, is in fact revolutionary since it suggests that the proper way to maintain a building is from capital and not from income and is the antithesis of the policies which, over the years, have done so much to preserve the integrity of historic fabric. Whether we choose to recognize it or not, a very large part of our appreciation of all sorts resides in our devotion to the picturesque. Writing in *Building and Prospects* in 1948 John Piper (through whose eyes this generation has learnt to see so much) referred to the quality which he described as 'pleasing decay' and made a plea for the preservation of the patina of ancient fabric: 'Once we get finally beyond our conventional reaction against the nineteenth century's enthusiasms and our distaste for the bad art that pleasing decay has nourished, we may be able to become ourselves again.' While allowing that there were no universally sensible policies in dealing with old buildings he went on to describe 'some warning echoes' as follows:

1. Perform the act with sensibility.
2. Ignore fashion and rely on the eyes.
3. Regard the present state of the building as possibly virtuous in itself.

The last of these three points is all-important if the textural quality and the picturesque are to be retained. The large offer does not allow of such restraint. The one-off restoration, with its avowed intention of making all secure in every possible contingency for a long period of time, has not time to consider the very quality which causes this or that building to comfort the human spirit.

Under a process of continuous care, on the other hand, mistakes can be made and mistakes can be rectified. The work that is not done this year can be done next year and the visual life of a building can develop and need not be subject to destructive shock therapy. The feeling that a historic building should be cared for as one would mend a piece of embroidery has a chance to flourish.

Following the successful effort of the Oxford University Historic Buildings Appeal Committee in the fifties and sixties, a sum of over £1,000,000 was raised and spent within a period of about five years on ancient college and university buildings. A scramble took place amongst all the colleges to get on the bus for it was accepted that this sensational offer could not be repeated.

Notwithstanding the excellence of much of the work that was done in these years, it is also true, as William Morris said in another context, that 'in the course of this double process of destruction and addition the whole surface of the building is necessarily tampered with; the appearance of antiquity is taken away from such old parts of the fabric as are left, and there is no laying to rest in the spectator the suspicion of what may have been lost; and, in short' (though not universally true) 'a feeble and lifeless forgery is the final result of all wasted labour'. No-one can, of course, blame the colleges or the university for this. The need was, indeed, an urgent one. Wildly spiralling costs following the compulsory years of neglect during the war had put the task beyond the scope of any traditional scheme of annual income expenditure. The owners of private houses had found the same thing and, though one may deplore the result in certain cases, though one may grieve for what has been lost, though one must learn the lesson and be glad of the opportunity to do so, it is, of course, as well that such a fund was available.

With the example of what happened in Oxford and with the memory of the Ecclesiological revolution at the end of the last century, enough has perhaps been said and shown to demonstrate that times of prosperity are not times in which the best work has been done and that the attitude of mind which has come to regard large capital sums as an essential pre-requisite for the processes of maintenance is one which we need to discard.

Churches, in the absence of income as such, have had to rely on other people's capital, but possibly the time is coming when they need no longer do so. For several years the Central Government has declared that an annual subsidy, now said to be £1,800,000, will be provided for the care of churches. Many have held that this is a derisory figure; in the diocese of St Edmundsbury and Ipswich alone it has been calculated that a sum of £3,000,000 is needed now to maintain the fabric of the historic churches in Suffolk. Suffolk is probably an exceptional case – a poor county but with a high proportion of the nation's wealth in church architecture. Against such a figure, under £2,000,000 for the whole country seems a spoonful indeed. There are forty-three dioceses in the country, giving on a capitation basis, a sum of £40,000 per annum to each. Treated as capital this is little enough but, regarded as income – annual income – the picture becomes more promising. Such a sum might become the sinews of care.

Inadequate to fund the 'great' restoration for which individual energy will still be required, here might well be the means over the years of gently but consistently not only controlling but directing the inevitable process of decay. Decay there will be. To suppose otherwise is to deny the fundamental fact of architectural life. If we are to admit the over-riding importance of the picturesque we allow that 'pleasing decay' has its place: we 'regard the present state of the building as possibly virtuous in itself'. To do otherwise is to resist the irresistible.

'No doubt within the last fifty years a new interest, almost like another sense, has arisen in these ancient monuments of art; and they have become the subject of one of the most interesting of studies, and of an enthusiasm, religious, historical, artistic, which is one of the undoubted gains of our time; yet we think that if the present treatment of them be continued, our descendants will find them useless for study and chilling to enthusiasm. We think that those last fifty years of knowledge and attention have done more for their destruction than all the foregoing centuries of revolution, violence and contempt.

'In early times this kind of forgery was impossible, because knowledge failed the builders, or perhaps because instinct held them back. If repairs were needed, if ambition or piety pricked on to change, that change was of necessity wrought in the unmistakable fashion of the time; a church of the eleventh century might be added to or altered in the twelfth, thirteenth, fourteenth, fifteenth, sixteenth, or even the seventeenth or eighteenth centuries; but every change, whatever history it destroyed, left history in the gap, and was alive with the spirit of the deeds done midst its fashioning.

'For what is left we plead before our architects themselves, before the official guardians of buildings, and before the public generally, and we pray them to remember how much is gone of the religion, thought and manners of time past, never, by almost universal consent, to be restored; and to consider whether it be possible to restore those buildings, the living spirit of which, it cannot be too often repeated, was an inseparable part of that religion and thought and those past manners.

'If, for the rest, it be asked us to specify what kind of amount of art, style, or other interest in a building makes it worth protecting, we answer, anything which can be looked on as artistic, picturesque, historical, antique, or substantial; any work, in short, over which educated, artistic people would think it worth while to argue at all.

'It is for all these buildings, therefore, of all times and styles, that we plead, and call upon those who have to deal with them to put protection in place of restoration, to stave off decay by daily care to prop a perilous wall or mend a leaky roof by such means as are obviously meant for support or covering, and show no pretence of other art, and otherwise to resist all tampering with either the fabric or ornament of the building as it stands.

'Thus, and thus only, shall we escape the reproach of our learning being turned into a snare to us; thus, and thus only, can we protect our ancient buildings and hand them down instructive and venerable to those that come after us.'

These are the words of William Morris in the Society for the Protection of Ancient Buildings *Manifesto*; the troubadour, the sweet singer, of a philosophy in which many of us spend our working lives really says all that there is to say.

PROBLEMS OF URBAN CHURCHES
by Canon Colin Scott

'Must there not be something wrong in a machinery so vast, so costly, so long sustained and so prominent, which yet produces results so startling in their meagreness?' – such was the view of a survey in the *Record* of 1888, 'South London: its religious condition, its needs and its hopes'. For years the Church of England has responded to the challenge of urban mission by multiplying parishes, building more churches and staffing them with clergy. However, these massive resources never really made an effective impact on working-class London. From the beginning these churches were mainly supported by the middle classes; as they moved out to the suburbs in the second half of the nineteenth century, small and dis-heartened congregations were left to maintain overlarge and ill-suited buildings with such help as dioceses could provide.

Nineteenth-century problems, however, have become literally ten times worse in the twentieth. In 1888 they lamented that less than 1 in 11 went to church on Sunday.

A survey in Battersea in 1964 showed an average main service attendance of under 1 in 110. Small congregations are due, in the main, to three factors. The first is falling population: the National Census figures for 1971 shows a decline to well under half the population figures returned in 1901 for most inner city areas. In some places, like Tower Hamlets, the population now is little more than a quarter that at the turn of the century. There has, of course, been some reduction over the same period in the number of parish churches but, on average, each inner city parish has appreciably fewer parishioners than in 1901.

The second factor is the disturbance due to massive redevelopment. Some of this was a consequence of bomb damage but in the main it is due to the concern of local authorities to revitalize depressed and overcrowded areas by widespread demolition and rebuilding. However good the intention the effect has often been to break up the community and to remove those members of con-gregations who had grown up within them and were ready to take a lead in church and local life. Linked with this is the difficulty young couples experience in finding accommodation in the area where they have lived as children.

Thirdly, the trend to increased secularization which affects the whole country has been most marked in urban areas. There is generally a decreasing fringe of well-wishers around any congregation in the inner city. This can lead to a sad polarization between a small local church largely preoccupied with its own survival and the wider community, centred on the Community Centre or Tenants Association, which regards the church as an irrelevance.

Such then are some of the difficulties confronting the congregation of an urban church. Sadly, their church building often constitutes an equally perplexing problem. Generally large, a little over one hundred years old, the church is regarded with a mixture of affection and frustration. Though loved for all it represents, it frequently constitutes a hindrance to real worship or effective mission. The reasons are financial, practical and social.

Fuel was cheap in Victorian England, so town churches are large, often seating 2,000, lofty and poorly insulated. Since the oil crisis many congregations find it impossible to heat their church in winter. Some shiver – one congregation I visited all arrived with hot-water bottles – others migrate to the church hall for the winter.

Many nineteenth-century London churches were built of Kentish ragstone. Although this stone is of variable quality in conditions of urban grime it seems to give trouble after about a hundred years. Many churches are now being faced with repairs to stonework costing £20,000–£30,000. Such repair bills are far beyond the means of a congregation which may only include 20–30 wage-earners.

Insurance also has become a financial burden. One South London parish with a modest congregation and a population of under 4,000 had their large Victorian church valued at a million pounds by their insurers. They were quoted an annual premium of a thousand pounds, though this was reduced somewhat after negotiation. The burden of this insurance was disproportionate to their ability or to their need; for if their church was destroyed they would have been content with a modest replacement at a fraction of the cost. Fortunately, more realistic and more flexible insurance cover is now being offered to meet such situations.

Quite apart from the cost, many congregations find their church building ill-suited to the needs of contemporary urban life. Too large for the congregation, cold, dilapidated and difficult to keep clean, the interior of many churches is in marked contrast to the homes of parishioners. Such churches convey neither the joy of worship nor the warmth of Christian fellowship to the newcomer. Committed Christians may bear discomfort stoically but visitors seldom come a second time. It is true that many Victorian churches, though of variable architectural quality, still have a certain townscape value. Yet even this may be largely undone where the church is left a gaunt and sooty survivor in an area of total redevelopment and proclaims to all a church which the world has passed by.

It is hardly surprising therefore that in such situations the local church often prefers to redevelop its buildings too, releasing surplus site for housing and providing new buildings suited to present-day needs. The Advisory Board for Redundant Churches in its 1975 report regretted 'that anti-preservationist pressures are to be found both within the Synod and amongst the Commissioners' but it is doubtful if those concerned for preservation always realize the burden this may be imposing on the local church.

Nonetheless there are many cases where conservation can make good pastoral sense. Where the outer fabric is sound an imaginative remodelling of the interior of a church may provide both a more modest place of worship and a whole range of provision for the needs of the local community. It is tragic if such true conservation is jeopardized by a preservationist objection to the alteration of the interior. In some cases this has led ultimately to the redundancy and possible demolition of the whole building. There will

be yet other cases where the need for the church building has passed, where depopulation makes it truly surplus. Here if no alternative use is found the true and courageous course may well be to demolish, sell the site and use the proceeds to build again where the people now live on a new estate, so that the church may be where her ministry is most needed.

REPAIR NOT RESTORATION
by John Schofield

The restorer's work is change: that arch-restorer Viollet-le-Duc says 'To restore a building is not to preserve it, repair or rebuild it; it is to reinstate it in a condition of completeness which could never have existed at any given time.' A restorer imposes his hypothesis of how a building was on the building as it is – so even the most conscientious restorations provoke the doubts of other experts. The result must be dogmatic; it is a process of a substitution which destroys its own provenance and cannot be reversed.

Repairers do not feel like that about old buildings: they are not so aggressive. Repair is a matter of response, of accepting the actuality of a building, of being modest for a while. It follows delight in what the building is, and the wish to share this delight. For the repairer the present is vital; he realizes that nothing can be made to last for ever and he has a natural abhorrence for the restorer's compound lie of immortality through copying copies of copies. . . . Artists and repairers have more constructive things to do than rehashing other people's work.

The idea of restoration is based on the premise that art can be copied. But it is through art that these miraculous old churches transcend everyday experience; the spirit and art of their builders suffuse every detail. By this artistic magic of personal communication, time is defied and sensations of real and present experience are amplified. How could this survive copying? Such things are unique, the result of circumstances which are obviously unrepeatable – personality, aspiration, mood, touch, culture, epoch. What way is there to equip ourselves with these and so complete what they produced?

We curse the Victorians for their sweeping restorations. Although these are often works of greater learning and conviction than today's efforts, they are, by general agreement, monstrously insensitive all the same. The Victorians were thorough; they demolished and rebuilt whole chunks of churches for stylistic conformity. Outright destruction on that scale, for whatever reason, would be rare today. Nor would we countenance the removal of a fifteenth-century window from a thirteenth-century church – not, that is, for the restoration of thirteenth-century completeness. But, if the old window offends by its too obvious marks of age, however structurally sound it is, it will be replaced by a copy sharp and smooth. You see, our restorers share with the Victorians, and all other restorers for that matter, a disregard for the real and noble signs of age often amounting to hatred – why else destroy ancient fabric which is structurally sound? Ours is an insidious corruption, just as active but less focused than that of the Victorians. It is the compulsion to tinker with every square inch of ancient surface: a few worn mediaeval sculptures supplanted this summer, the nave roof 'picked out' by someone with tins of red and blue and green and, of course, gold in time for Christmas, the Elizabethan tomb figures scoured and redecorated the following spring. The result is a show of dazzling brightness and completeness with the reassuring knowledge of antiquity safely out of sight, and the justification that originally also all must have been new and bright and complete. Out go mystery, subtelty, profundity, sympathy. And with them spirituality too.

These are the proclivities of the mid-twentieth-century restorers. In case there should be doubt as to the damage they are doing, I will cite a few examples: at the great church of Fairford in Gloucestershire weathered carvings of animals on the labels of the window hoodmoulds have been cut away and copies put back. The famous little Climbing Boy has been taken down from the string course and the delightful humour of his situation turned into a silly lavatory joke by his replacement. In celebration of the six hundredth anniversary of Wellow church near Bath, the ancient heads of king and bishop beside the tower doorway have been chopped out and are supplanted by dreary reminders of the restoration patron and his bishop. A West Country speciality is the painting-up of roofs – an outrageously gaudy example is the once-splendid tie-beam roof of St Cuthbert's, Wells. Here the colours used are almost fluorescent. At St Mary's, Taunton and Evercreech in Somerset, Ottery St Mary in Devon, St Ives, Cornwall and many another, such attempts at restoring colouring on roofs and screens have destroyed the planes of the carving and blurred the design. At Colyton in Devon Jacobean monumental sculpture in the Pole Chapel is under restoration. The original painting on the magnificent architectural monument to John and Elizabeth Pole is said to be too delicate for cleaning and conservation. Instead of being left alone at least, the paint is to be stripped back to the stone and the whole edifice recoloured from analysis of the destroyed material and comparison with other monuments of the period. Such effigies are both ancient sculptures and ancient paintings too – and very subtle works they often are. Would a reputable gallery clean off the flaking face of a seventeenth-century portrait for the sake of restoring it 'complete' again from the evidence so discovered?

The tendency is always to make an ancient building less, to reduce what it has to say. Archaeologists seek what it hides; restorers try putting back what isn't there – and so obscure what is; stonecarvers cut out what is there to insert something different and tourists have only got time for superficiality anyway. All set demands on the building and each, if let loose, subtracts from its value to the rest.

The only way which I can see towards the ideal of not reducing old buildings, is through response instead of imposition; repair not restoration. Let each repair affirm the reality of the ancient building itself. That way also the possibility of every interest is entertained.

Why, if this is so, is the repairer's attitude so particularly hated by certain vicars, deans and so many church architects? We are not the ones who want to see our ancient church art and imagery changed; in truth ours is an utterly uncontentious view. We want to let old churches, in all their many riches of art and intellect and spirit, speak for themselves.

PART THREE
SOLUTIONS PAST & PRESENT

CHURCH AND STATE
by Nicholas Cooper

The Church of England has always been a state within a state. From the early Middle Ages – from long before Thomas Becket – the Church always asserted its independence of the government. Since the Reformation, both have had the same legal head, the Crown, and each has sometimes tried to use the other's powers for its own purposes. But in the eighteenth century, the government was content to let the Church go its own way, and in the nineteenth the Church of England was enjoying a revival. It was keen to stress its independence from the secular power, and though the state might occasionally legislate on forms of worship and Church government, that was as far as its interference was allowed to extend.

It is true that as early as the 1830s and 1840s there were a few who called for state involvement in the care of churches and cathedrals, but this was for the most part a belated response to the Church's neglect of its buildings in the previous century. Questions were asked in the Commons about the opening of cathedrals to the public (in those days they were only open at certain times and on payment to the vergers) and even suggestions made for the appointment of a National Monuments Commission that would look after historic buildings and cathedrals, and give money and advice for their care. (There was already such a body in France.) But in the light of the views then current on what were the acceptable limits of state intervention, no government could seriously contemplate such a scheme. In any case the Anglican authorities would have resisted such a proposal just as strongly then as they were to do later.

It was only in Ireland that in the nineteenth century the government took any action over ancient church buildings. The Irish Church Disestablishment Bill of 1869 originally provided for the government's giving financial help towards the maintenance of six major Irish churches

and cathedrals that were to remain in use for worship but which it was feared would decay for lack of funds. In the event, the Roman Catholics objected to the spending of taxpayers' money on Protestant churches, while the Protestants were afraid that government money would be followed by state control. Gladstone, the Prime Minister, did not feel strongly about the proposal, and the clause was dropped, but the debate is an interesting rehearsal of some of the arguments about state aid that have been heard much more recently.

But the Act that became law in that year did contain another clause that anticipated some recent proposals. This effected the transfer of over a hundred ruins that had been Church property into the hands of the Irish Office of Works for preservation. In view of the Church of England's continuing responsibility for a large number of ruined churches, the initiative of 1869 is perhaps worth remembering.

It was not until early in the twentieth century that the question of state control of Anglican buildings was seriously proposed, and by then, as in the 1840s, it was in response to a situation that was already largely historic. The Victorian restoration of churches and cathedrals had often been ruthless and insensitive, and while in 1877 the Society for the Protection of Ancient Buildings had been founded to put a stop to what William Morris called a 'torrent of destructiveness', many people felt that additional controls were needed. Anyone who wanted to tamper with the fabric of a church had to apply to the chancellor of the diocese for a faculty that granted him permission (this is still the case) but under the law as it then stood the chancellor had no concern with the artistic merits of the application, only with the legality of what was proposed. And cathedrals were – and still are – completely a law to themselves: the dean of each cathedral has sole

201. Bury St Edmunds, Suffolk; former Unitarian chapel. Now in the care of the Department of the Environment

control over what happens in his building, and nobody, not even the bishop, can stop him doing what he likes with it. It was this situation that led to demands for the inclusion of cathedrals, at least, within the mechanisms of control set up by the Ancient Monuments Bill of 1913.

It was, however, the failure to have church buildings included in the scope of the 1913 Act that is the origin of the so-called 'ecclesiastical exemption' of church buildings from the state's historic building controls. A high-powered delegation, led by Lord Curzon, waited on Archbishop Randall Davidson to urge on him the value of the expert advice that could be given by the Office of Works experts if they were granted the powers to give it. The delegation stressed, too, the deplorable results that sometimes still followed from uninformed restoration work in churches. Davidson, however, was adamant. Churches were for worship, not for antiquarians, and it was not to be expected in that age that Parliament would vote against the express wishes of the Archbishop of Canterbury. Subsequent legislation, notably successive Town and Country Planning Acts, has provided ever stronger legal protection for historic buildings, but ecclesiastical buildings are still exempted from such control.

As a result of the discussions of 1913, however, the Church of England did ultimately establish advisory committees in each diocese, to comment on the artistic and architectural merits of work proposed for churches, and before a faculty is granted these bodies must now be consulted. A national organization was also set up (now the Council for Places of Worship) to guide the diocesan committees and to co-ordinate attitudes on artistic matters. These bodies generally work well, and have done much to disarm criticism of the Church of England's treatment of its fine buildings. But a situation has now arisen that was unforeseen in 1913 or for many years after that. The problem now is not of the proper care of churches that are still well supported, but of the preservation of churches that are unwanted.

The problem is not totally new: a few churches in the City of London, for instance, were pulled down by Acts of Parliament in the last century. But redundancy on a large scale, resulting from shifting populations and declining church membership, is a feature of the last thirty years. And while the energies of the Church of England have been largely directed towards new forms of ministry and of ritual, public appreciation of old buildings of all kinds has been growing fast. The position became one of public support for official involvement in the preservation of churches, with the Church of England ready to accept help

202. Studley Royal, Yorkshire; St Mary. William Burges' ecclesiastical masterpiece, looked after by the Department of the Environment

203. Shotley, Northumberland; St Andrew. Church, mausoleum and hearse house, now vested in the Redundant Churches Fund

204. Skidbrooke, Lincolnshire; St Botolph. Alone on the flat marsh, with trees its only company, now vested in the Redundant Churches Fund

205. Friarmere, Yorkshire; St Thomas. Eighteenth-century vernacular classical, now vested in the Redundant Churches Fund

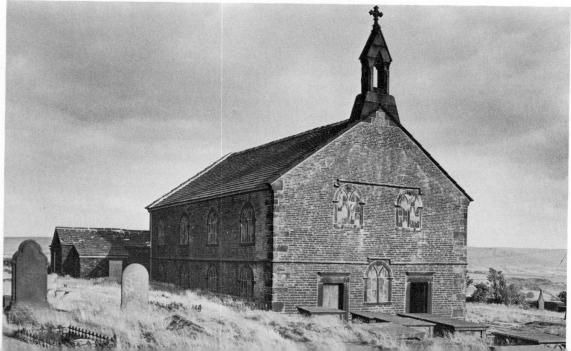

– and possibly some control – over matters no longer so central to its contemporary pastoral responsibilities.

It was to meet this situation that in 1958 a committee was set up under Lord Bridges to consider how redundant churches of distinction could be preserved, and how their merits could be properly considered when they were taken out of parochial use. The Bridges Committee reported in 1960, and its recommendations were closely followed in the procedures for dealing with redundant churches that were established by the 1968 Pastoral Measure.

These procedures are complicated. Briefly, the Pastoral Measure established two new bodies, an Advisory Board for Redundant Churches and a Redundant Churches Fund. A redundant church which the Advisory Board recommends for preservation, and for which no acceptable alternative use can be found (and for the best churches there can be no other acceptable use) is normally vested by the Church Commissioners in the Redundant Churches Fund for permanent preservation. The Fund derives its income partly from the Commissioners, partly from the sale of the sites of redundant churches that are expendable, and partly from the state through the Department of the Environment. The principle of state involvement in the preservation of redundant churches is thus already acted upon.

It is possible, moreover, for a redundant church to pass into the care of the Department of the Environment itself, and two churches of great historic and archaeological importance have already done so (in August 1976). But the problem of ruined churches is so far entirely unresolved. The Church of England owns hundreds of ruined churches which need special techniques for their preservation. The Department of the Environment, with its long experience of caring for ancient monuments, is the natural custodian of these, but the state is understandably, unwilling to assume what could ultimately become a large additional responsibility.

There remains, too, the problem of paying for the upkeep and repair of churches that still have a congregation. There are innumerable fine churches that are still in use but which face disproportionately large problems of maintenance. In 1975 the government announced that it was prepared, in principle, to make a grant of up to £1,000,000 at 1973 prices for the maintenance of churches in use. This money would probably be administered by the Historic Buildings Council which since 1953 has been making substantial annual grants out of public funds for the repair of secular buildings. But the precise terms and conditions on which grants are to be made have not at the time of writing been finalized, and there seems no possibility of any cash actually being available before 1978. And it is not known whether the traditional exemption of Anglican churches from normal historic building controls will be perpetuated.

206. Croome d'Abitot, Worcestershire; St Mary Magdalen. Built by Capability Brown and Robert Adam, containing the splendid monuments of the Coventry family, now vested in the Redundant Churches Fund

Discussion so far has been mainly about the buildings of the Church of England – these, of course, constitute by far the largest number and the most ancient of ecclesiastical buildings in this country. But other denominations also have chapels and churches of historic importance, and government aid, when it is eventually forthcoming, will be available for buildings of all sects. On the other hand, while the Church of England can, by virtue of the Pastoral Measure and of acts of Parliament, demolish its historic churches without listed building consent, other denominations cannot. They do not require consent to the alteration of a historic building in use for worship, but they do for total demolition. The situation is in several ways anomalous, but until the need for fresh legislation has been clearly shown it is unlikely that the state will do anything to change the situation that presently obtains.

Whatever the ultimate conditions under which state aid will be granted to historic churches, at least it is now recognized on all sides that the church authorities can no longer afford to bear the sole burden of maintaining their historic buildings, and that these buildings are now appreciated by many thousands of people who never visit them for worship. Church and state are agreed that old churches are a matter of public concern; it is only the Church's traditional independence, and central government's present lack of money, that has so long delayed their more closely working together in a common interest.

208. Portland, Dorset; St George Reforne. A complete eighteenth-century interior with twin pulpits, now vested in the Redundant Churches Fund

207. Parracombe, North Devon; St Petrock. One of some 100 churches vested in the Redundant Churches Fund

NEW USES FOR CHURCHES
by Patrick Brown

The 1976 Conference of the Evangelical Church in Germany was held in the Gothic Brüderkirche in Kassel. About 300 delegates attended to discuss the theme 'Using Space', and it was entirely appropriate that this great disused church should have served as their base: within the three days of the meeting the building was used for lectures, discussions, exhibitions, displays, meals, music, dance and religious celebration. By means of elegant suspended 'sails' the otherwise poor acoustics were corrected, and a series of easily moved and impressively uncomplicated plywood screens made for varied spaces and seating arrangements. The occasion was a live demonstration of the way in which a redundant church might be put to imaginative and fruitful use with the minimum of cost, alteration, and effort.

Many countries face the problem of dealing with unwanted churches, but the Church of England is probably the only organization systematically attempting to protect its buildings from unseemly disfigurement or unwarranted demolition once they are no longer required by their worshipping communities. Since the introduction of the Pastoral Measure in 1968 the Church Commissioners have declared redundant well over 500 churches. Of these, about one third are likely to be demolished, one fifth vested in the Redundant Churches Fund, and the remainder – nearly half of the total – offered for suitable alternative use. Arguments for and against re-use include practical, aesthetic, financial, theological and emotional issues, but there is active encouragement for re-use proposals of great variety, and a small number of worthwhile conversions has been completed. It is to be hoped that many more schemes will follow, since we must not allow the design skills, energies and resources invested in these buildings in the past to be swept away in wanton destruction on the scale which is happening to secular buildings; also there are often convincing arguments for retaining such significant buildings both as elements of value in the landscape or town scene, and as focal community memories.

In considering re-use for churches there are two major contentious issues. One is the suitability of a proposed new use; the other is the acceptability of structural or architectural change to the building. A first assessment is desirable to establish whether *any* new use is justifiable, or whether the church is of such quality architecturally or historically as to warrant recommendation to the Redundant Churches Fund. The limited finances of the Fund, and reluctance of many churchmen and others to hold buildings apparently unused in this way impose limitations on this as a solution.

Where alternative use is postulated, alterations to the outside of the building should always be minimal, but there will also be many cases where the interior is of high architectural value, so that little or no subdivision or modification should be made to it. If so, there are new functions which can be considered. Most obvious is to see whether another worshipping community would appreciate the building: the Greek Orthodox Church and the Roman Catholics for instance have each taken over a number of former Anglican churches, and in Bristol William Butterfield's Highbury Congregational Chapel has been adopted by the Anglicans to replace a nearby but over-large urban church designed by Piers St Aubyn. Museums, concert and recital rooms, and display galleries are also appropriate functions for consideration in these circumstances. The much used St John's, Smith Square, is perhaps the best known (though a bombed rather than formally redundant church), but the splendid ecclesiastical museum in St Nicholas, Bristol may also be cited. Here a gallery has been inserted in the renovated shell of this

210. Chichester, Sussex; St Andrew. Before and after conversion, now a centre for the arts

211. Colchester, Essex; St Giles. Now a Freemasons hall

212. Edinburgh; St George, Charlotte Square. Section before conversion, and after, showing conversion for use

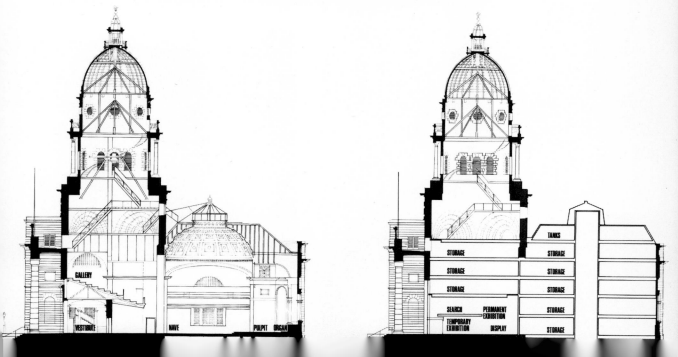

213. Edinburgh; Trinity Church. The City Library newspaper room

215. Norwich; St Peter Hungate. Now an ecclesiastical museum

214. York; St Sampson. An old people's day centre

216. Hastings, Sussex; St Mary in the Castle. Used by another denomination

bombed eighteenth-century church in the heart of the city, but the whole space of the original is clearly seen from the main floor. The new work has been undertaken with care, and a certain luxuriousness is conveyed by a rich purple carpet overall. The scheme is a demonstration of the virtues of flexibility, since although this is primarily a museum to display the church treasures of the diocese the city's history is also explained, and island fittings can be unplugged from power sources and pushed to the sides so that the main floor can be used for recitals and meetings. At St Peter in the East, Oxford, a fine mediaeval church has become the library to St Edmund Hall, and is a good illustration of how a new function may be assimilated in a space of strong architectural quality not only without harming it, but even enhancing it. The virtues of the original space are complemented by the new bookcases and fittings in a building which seems to provide admirable environmental conditions for quiet reading and research. Not far away, in the High Street, the former All Saints' is now also a library – for Lincoln College – and a concrete floor was successfully inserted over a newly excavated crypt in the classical structure. A more modest adaptation of a church without structural alteration or subdivision is the Arts Centre in the former Holy Trinity, Wareham, Dorset, undertaken by a private enthusiast; abutting one of the principal streets, its square tower remains part of the town's waterside skyline, and the visitor enjoys the complete two-aisled space when looking at the paintings displayed for sale.

Often the interior characteristics of the churches are not of sufficient merit to justify unmodified retention, so that a wider range of uses can be contemplated, with subdivision to offer extra floor space or required privacy. In these cases the Advisory Board for Redundant Churches has a brief to safeguard architectural and historic qualities, and to ensure that any new work is undertaken to appropriately high architectural standards. The impact of the Measure's procedures, moderated through the Board, may be judged from completed schemes such as those below.

The nineteenth-century church of St Thomas, Southgate, Winchester, was converted for use as the Hampshire Record Office. The interior was not architecturally important, but it has a prominent spire important to the city's image. As a result, the building is practically unaltered outside, but inside new concrete floors and fire-resistant walls have been built so that St Thomas now securely houses valuable archives which can also be studied by researchers and conserved by staff in the various spaces available. If the alternative to such re-use is demolition surely such restructuring is entirely justified?

An enterprising variation of the 'lost interior' theme is the Regimental Museum of the Green Howards at Richmond, Yorkshire, attractively housed in the market place church of Holy Trinity. Upper parts of the original arcading now serve as glass-fronted display cases, and the timber roof can be studied at close quarters. The work, which was carried through energetically by the regiment, was assisted by a grant from the English Tourist Board, and – a generous gesture by the promoters – the east end is still retained as a chapel for use by parishioners.

Whilst a re-used warehouse might without question be restructured as a casino or a bank, could uses of this kind be construed as suitable in a former church? There is, in fact, an example of a former garrison church in Hamlin now used as a bank, and presumably if churches are to become community centres (again!), there is a probability that mild forms of gambling such as bingo will take place in them. This perhaps illustrates the difficulty of determining a line of acceptability. The Anglicans have ruled against some specific proposals for alternative use: once against use as a mosque, and once where a Masonic temple was proposed. There is nearly general agreement on uses which benefit the community, and open the building to the serious visitor (re-use will often render the building more accessible than in its days as a locked church!). Hence the museum, concert hall, or community centre is especially appropriate, both on this score, and in terms of kindness to the fabric, but many other functions also meet the criterion, as, for instance, in St Sampson, York, converted to an old persons' day centre. Here new floors and partitions provide enclosures, but in such a way that all new work could be later removed without harming the original.

The same strategy has been used in All Saints, Dorchester for the Dorset Natural History and Archaeological Society. This is another nineteenth-century church whose spire, of Portland stone, forms a vital part of the townscape, and credit is due to both town and county for raising £7,000 towards repair costs, as well as to the private museum organization prepared to take over and maintain the building hereafter. Furthermore, without generous terms from the Church Commissioners the whole enterprise might have failed. This example, like the Heritage Centres at York (St Mary, Castlegate) and Chester (St Michael), is a further example of retention of the building allied to renewed accessibility for the public. A further modest case worth quoting is the re-use of All Saints, Pallant, Chichester, West Sussex, as a local Red Cross headquarters. A single-cell thirteenth-century building, visible from and close to one of the main arteries

217. Langdon Hills, Essex; All Saints. Transformed into a house

218. Newton in the Willows, Northamptonshire; St Faith. Now a field centre; the chancel serves as a laboratory

219. Bristol; St Nicholas Church and City Museum. A concert in progress

of the city, it has been subdivided to give one large and one smaller space, plus small offices in an annexe, but it is a pity that the wall memorial tablets have been covered and hidden from view in an otherwise sensible transformation. There must be scope for many more adaptations of this calibre, inexpensive by comparison with new premises and closely related to the former use of the building.

Because of the numbers of people in an urban catchment area, and the varied functions which a town is able to sustain, it ought normally to be possible to find some alternative use for an urban church. But what of the many country churches becoming redundant in dioceses like Lincoln, Salisbury, or Hereford? Whilst a few may become specialist localized museums, or perhaps serve as bases for music festivals (as Boughton Aluph for Stour Festival), for the most part the rural churches must look for functions more suited to their location. They do have important advantages – attractive sites, superb views and surroundings, an 'isolating' private zone provided by a surrounding churchyard. Field centre or pilgrimage centre, or house; this is the special appeal and re-use area to seek. The use of outstations from which school groups can make local studies is well established, and the idea can be extended so that ornithologists, archaeologists, or local working parties can share costs and facilities, as well as spreading the number of hours of use in a week; as a consequence, costs of maintenance can also be spread. A former chapel at Chadkirk, on the edge of the Greater Manchester area where it meets the country, has been adapted for community use in this sense, and at Newton-in-the-Willows, near Kettering, Northamptonshire, the former St Faith's church is a field centre for study of local history, geography, natural history and other subjects. In addition to spaces for discussions, library, dining, and a laboratory, an inserted gallery also gives accommodation for up to ten students in two small dormitories.

Some small country churches were built as private manor chapels, and there is scope for them to be returned to private ownership. In the Salisbury diocese Tarrant Rawston, Upcerne, Bryanston, and Hanford have been redisposed in this way – the last two as school chapels.

The surest way to rouse agitated local opinion against re-use of a country church is to suggest that it might become a house. Although this is understandable, those who oppose such a change must realize that, unless they can offer a viable alternative, with suitable financing for conversion and maintenance, the implication is that the church will have to be demolished. Local planning authorities must also be made aware of the risks of refusing permission for church-to-house change, often made on the grounds that

no more development is permitted in a village, or that services are inadequate; where an authority is not opposed in principle to the idea, they ought to be encouraged to give a blessing at the outline stage.

Certainly the use of small churches as houses demands a special approach to lay-out and use of space: the most acceptable solution will often be a large studio space with lesser functions in galleries. The essence ought to be to retain an exterior as fully as possible, and to structure the interior so that its original qualities can still be savoured. Perhaps the best illustration so far of this philosophy is in the former church of St Mary, Langdon Hills, Essex, where the new owner with his architect has undertaken the minimum of change to provide himself with a fine church house. Another worthy example is in St Nicholas, Barway, near Ely, where a surprising amount has been achieved in the confines of the former chapel.

Other rural possibilities include the 'stabilized ruin', with attendant picnic area, as at Clophill, Bedfordshire; the rural craft training centre, as in the Orton Centre, Northamptonshire, where masonry apprentices whilst learning their craft have also helped to repair the little church; a village hall, as proposed for Bickenhall, Somerset; and, in a suitable accessible and overseen position, a church as a diocesan furniture store for temporarily housing pews and other fittings from re-dundant churches, as at Kingston Blount, Oxfordshire.

Because of the cut back in local government funds, there is a degree of despondency at present about re-using these churches. Undoubtedly cash is one of the keys to success, but the major requirements are the initial will and continued enthusiasm, imagination, and cash – in that order. Continuation of the control system exercised by the Commissioners is essential, but in addition a proper method of supervision and maintenance of the buildings during the statutory waiting period (of up to three years) is needed. At present there is considerable unwarranted loss through vandalism and natural decline because Diocesan Boards of Finance – understandably – are reluctant to commit funds to maintenance of surplus plant. However, in the long run this is unsound book-keeping, since well-maintained buildings are obviously more valuable assets than decaying ones.

Although this essay has related principally to the changes taking place through the Pastoral Measure, it seems clear that a broader oversight is needed, covering all churches or religious buildings in a town or region, so that conflicting claims can be better balanced, waste of resources reduced, and the nation's great wealth of church and chapel buildings more meaningfully conserved.

CHURCHES RESTORED
by Peter Burman

No one who visits churches as a regular part of his existence can doubt that the overwhelming majority are remarkably well cared for and loved. Those who have been visiting them for much longer lives than mine add also that churches are cared for today as never before and that it is much more uncommon than it was – say between the wars – to find a church which shows all the signs of having been abandoned by those responsible for it. How true is that, I wonder?

One has the impression that more people go to church in the villages than in the towns and cities – glance through the figures in the *Diocesan Handbook* of a rural diocese in England, for example, and the smaller the population the higher the proportion, or so it seems, of those who are on the electoral roll. And more strenuous efforts are made now than used to be the case to keep electoral rolls up to date. Ask how many, out of a population of two or three hundred, go to church regularly to worship, and you may be told 'about a dozen'. But there is a curious principle whereby many families send a representative, so to speak, and when that particular member of the family dies or perhaps moves elsewhere she or he is replaced by someone else. The ripple of involvement which this represents is of some significance, for it is by no means an otiose idea that the parish church belongs not solely to those who use it as a place of worship but to the whole community. The results can be seen in some of the examples which follow.

In England, a major factor in ensuring the preservation of historic churches – and by 'historic' I mean those of any age which, on artistic grounds, are worth bothering about at all – has been the Church of England's Inspection of Churches Measure 1955. Just as the Faculty Jurisdiction, which dates from the mid-thirteenth century, may be said to have anticipated the principles of listed building control by some 700 years, so the Inspection of Churches Measure

was ahead of its time in realizing that regular compulsory inspection by a suitably qualified architect made sense in terms of preserving the building and, ultimately, in saving money. 'Stave off decay by daily care' said William Morris, and no one has ever given better advice with regard to our custodianship of buildings, whatever their age, but specially significant when dealing with a building which, by its nature, its materials, its vulnerability through age, and the artistic value which it enshrines, is tender and needs particularly sensitive treatment. The Measure in question was the recommendation of a Commission set up by the Church of England to consider what steps needed to be taken to ensure the survival of churches in many cases still at that time catching up on the backlog of repairs caused by the last World War. An architect, approved as appropriate for that particular church by the Diocesan Advisory Committee (DAC) for the Care of Churches, carries out an inspection at intervals not longer than every five years, and his report then serves – not as a specification, which it quite definitely is not – as the basis for a programme of care and conservation extending over the next five years, with a glimpse into the future at longer-term needs, like the re-pointing of a tower (unspectacular, expensive, but vital about once every hundred years) or the re-laying of a roof, items which need long preparation and probably a good deal of saving up before they can be tackled.

In 1953 the Historic Churches Preservation Trust was established, to raise money and make grants to important historic churches of whatever denominations. In the twenty-five years since its founding the Trust has raised the astonishingly large sum, for a small private body with a single executive officer and a modest amount of secretarial help, of £2½ million, which it has disbursed in grants to some 3,000 churches, preference being given on the whole

220. Tue Brook, Liverpool; St John the Baptist. G. F. Bodley 1868–70; successful revival of decorative scheme by C. E. Kempe carried out by Campbell, Smith & Co.

to the large mediaeval churches in relatively small villages with very little hope of raising enormous sums for themselves.

But 'very little hope', did I say? The evidence seems to show that it is not the size of a population (and certainly not the size of the congregation!), or its apparent wealth, that is significant in the raising of money but the morale and determination of key people, who are either the natural leaders in the community or who are prepared to become so. In 1965, the parish of Worstead in Norfolk – a parish with a population of 753 (electoral roll membership 53) – appointed as their architect a young Norwich architect, who made a careful examination of this enormous and particularly splendid church and found that something like £40,000 to £50,000 needed to be spent in the next five to ten years. Now the maximum amount of help from outside, the expectation from out-of-the-parish sources might have been something like this:

(a) £1,000 from the Historic Churches Preservation Trust, with perhaps an interest-free loan of a further £1,000, and possibly a sum in the order of about £300–£500 from an affiliated county Historic Churches Trust

(b) £200 from the Incorporated Church Building Society

(c) £200 'as a token' from the District Council

(d) £1,000 from a private donor having connections with the parish

(e) £500 from the diocese, if the parish was lucky, or possibly a loan.

In all, a parish may be exceedingly fortunate if it succeeds in netting any more than about £3,000 in straightforward grants. (These are not the grants received at Worstead, but on a typical scale.) A parish can, generally speaking, do one of two things in such a situation: it can lie down and pretend that nothing has happened, and postpone any real action *sine die*; it can make a superhuman effort and triumph over all odds. The second is what Worstead did: eleven years after the bombshell of realizing that so much work needed to be done £80,000 has been raised and spent – inflation having taken its usual toll of the original estimate – and the parish is cheerfully raising the next £10,000 and will then doubtless go on to raise the next £15,000. Much of the work is what I have previously described as unspectacular – repointing of the massive and lofty tower, with all the expensive scaffolding that entails; recasting and re-laying all the lead roofs; provision of new water disposal system and drainage. All these are the very basic necessities of historic buildings and maintenance; and though they may not be spectacular, the consequences of neglecting them may well be disastrous – the recent

collapse of towers at Bildeston, Suffolk, and Hagworthingham, Lincolnshire, and the enforced demolition of the tower of Frating, Essex, show that this is no idle prospect. Many of the flint towers of Norfolk and Suffolk are badly in need of repointing and it is the kind of repair work that is neglected at our peril.

So what did the parish of Worstead do? After a great deal of planning it launched one carefully considered activity after another, drawing in practically the whole of the population. In the Middle Ages, Worstead was famous for its cloth, and now ladies of the parish sit at their looms in the north aisle of the church and make beautiful fabrics both to adorn the church and for sale to the public, who (drawn by publicity in the local press and on television) come to see the cloth being made. Publicity is important, if a venture of this kind is to succeed, but it should if possible be the kind of spontaneous publicity which results from doing something really worthwhile. Once a year there is the Worstead Fair, which in 1976 raised almost £4000 nett. People come to the Fair from all over Norfolk and – taking into account those on holiday in the county – from much further afield. The quality of publications – guide books, postcards, reproductions of brasses – is exceptionally good and it is therefore possible to spend a pound or so on really good 'merchandise'; not only is the 'message' thereby disseminated but the visitor has something worthwhile to take away with him.

The same sense of 'taking trouble' is evident at Edington Priory church, Wiltshire, which has also raised more than £40,000 in the past ten years and – having put the fabric into excellent repair, and conserved (with the help of grants) several outstanding monuments, and the stained glass – is now setting about the provision of a new organ, and a new heating system. (Too many parishes, alas, have been known to begin with the organ and the heating while the rain pours through the roof.) Since 1962 there has been a Festival of Cathedral Music, when a choir (or two choirs) sings the *Opus Dei* for a week in a manner which no cathedral can nowadays afford to keep up, living in houses in the village, or camping in a field. Special musical events are also mounted, and the church is packed evening after evening during the Festival. A smaller but surprisingly large congregation comes every morning to the sung Eucharist, with music by Lassus, or Palestrina, or Byrd, or Vaughan Williams.

There is an enormous potential for well prepared worship and music-making in our parish churches and in our chapels. But, it may be said, these things are all very well in attractive country parishes but the same recipe will not work in London or Glasgow or Bangor or Manchester,

221. Gorton, Manchester; Our Lady and St Thomas. Sir Walter Tapper, 1925. Redecoration of the interior 1976, with new floor and new lighting and reglazing of windows; stalls from The Saviour, Bolton

222. Deptford, South London; St Paul. Thomas Arthur, completed 1730. Spectacular plasterwork and woodwork cleaned and conserved 1975–6

223. Rochester, Kent; St Nicholas. Church of 1624, part kept as a church and part converted into diocesan office and SPCK bookshop, stonework repaired and interior redecorated

for every place has its *genius loci* and its possibilities. Consider the recent history of Holy Trinity, Upper Tooting, a South London suburb which no one, for all its qualities, has suggested to be a significant part of our heritage. Three years ago the church was clearly in difficult straits: the tower and stonework needed £20,000 worth of repointing, the parish hall was on the point of collapse, the roofs needed mending, and so on. A new vicar came and assessed the situation in consultation with the diocese: it would be possible to demolish the hall and the church and start again, using the proceeds from the sale of one site to redevelop the other. (This used to be a very attractive and much sought-after solution while the property boom lasted, and much cursed were they who tried to argue against it.) However, not only did such a solution have its weak points – which emerged in the course of deliberation – but the church, and particularly the tower, were recognized as having something very definite to contribute to the townscape of Trinity Road, a major highway. Moreover, the building spoke a witness to the Christian faith, and to the continuity of that faith, far more vividly than that could be provided by a new building within their means. So, the solution was to sell the hall, and not the church; to convert the south aisle, which might have been designed for such a conversion, into the hall, with all the necessary facilities for looking after people during the weekdays as well as after services, and the tower was repaired. Much was done by voluntary labour, especially on the hall conversion, and £23,000 was raised by the sale of the hall; but £11,000 had to be raised by the parish, and every parishioner was personally visited – and a visit can mean a great deal in pastoral terms, reaching out as it does to the old, the lonely and the bed-sitterdom – the problem explained in a circular, and a further visit made to see if the parishioner was willing to contribute. And two separate 'talent schemes' raised about £1,000 apiece – a certain number of parishioners being given, say, £1 and the challenge being to turn it into £10, or £15, or £50.

To take another urban example, also in South London, St Paul's, Deptford, is one of the great Baroque churches of England – designed by Thomas Archer, and built in the time of Deptford's maritime prosperity. With ruthless redevelopment, a good deal of unemployment, and a constantly changing population it must have seemed as unpromising a place as any in which to teach people the Christian faith, indeed to get them to come anywhere near the church at all. Yet, some seven years after the arrival of the present incumbent, there are rarely less than 200 at the Parish Mass on Sunday mornings, the crypt is a most exciting place where the elderly of the parish are able to join a lunch club, play bingo, and enjoy themselves, while the youth of the parish use it for a discotheque in the evenings – and the church has been splendidly and painstakingly restored, a symbol of the new spirit which is rising Phoenix-like in Deptford, at a cost of £200,000. The Borough of Lewisham gave £25,000 – surely an unprecedented amount for a local authority to give a parish church.

The emphasis here has been on churches which are still in use as parish churches, and we must plan firmly for the fact that – whatever gloomy prophets may say, and however sternly they look only on one side of the coin – the majority of our churches will stay in use for their original purpose. A word must here be said, however, about the work of the Redundant Churches Fund established jointly by the State and the Church of England in 1969, whose example we might hope to see followed sooner rather than later by other denominations and by the Churches in Wales and Scotland. The Fund's function is to be, in relation to the 100 or so churches in its care, as the National Trust is to the houses in its care, i.e. to put them, patiently and gradually, in good repair, arrange for their regular maintenance and supervision and to stimulate and (where necessary) guide the emergence of local committees to be responsible for the day-to-day management of the building. The more enterprising local bodies of Friends have organized concerts and exhibitions, made the church seem welcoming at all times, and ensured that a large body of enthusiastic and truly 'caring' people are present at the occasional services which the Fund likes to take place, at least on or near the Feast of Title of the church. In taking on responsibility for such a large number of churches – ranging from the tiny chapelry of Oborne, just outside Sherborne in Dorset, to the noble town churches of St Mary Quay, Ipswich, and St Peter, Sandwich in Kent – the Fund's praises deserve to be sung: not only has it achieved something of unique value in terms of the conservation of these buildings, preserving them intact with all their historic furnishings and contents, but the churches provide for the visitor an altogether special sort of experience. 'They are not dead, but sleep,' one might say; and yet, provided they are open and accessible they are by no means asleep for the visitors who respond to them. They are 'momentary monasteries', places of pilgrimage and spiritual refreshment, 'where prayer has been valid', in T. S. Eliot's words, and where 'the communication of the dead is a tongue with fire beyond the language of the living.'

CHURCHES ADAPTED
by Pamela Tudor-Craig

'I thrilled to see every square inch of the church building being used every hour of the day. There were normally between twenty and thirty people actually working in the building – and there were 30 telephones. One really felt that at last those old bricks were fully mobilized to glorify God and to serve the community.'
(Nicholas Stacey Who Cares *London 1971, p. 280)*
So wrote Nick Stacey of the last stage in his adaptations of St Mary's, Woolwich (begun 1961, architect Thomas Ford). By 1971 he was housing a restaurant, the Citizens' Advice Bureau, offices for the Council for Social Services and, in the crypt, a young people's club. In social terms his experiment was a success. In others he himself expressed disappointment. The weekday activities did not lead to a significant increase in Sunday attendance, disproving the theory that people did not come to church because, so to speak, they did not know the way up the path. Kenneth White has voiced the question behind the Woolwich approach in his pamphlet, *Centres for the Servants* (Bramcote, 1975): 'What kind of stewardship keeps an expensive building disused 95 per cent of the week?' To which I would respond with a corollary: 'How can anyone – priest, layworker, choirmaster – operate in a largely empty context without a sense of failure?' and also a counter question: 'Where else in a roaring city can a man hope to satisfy the hunger for space and silence in which to find God – if not in a church?' Nicholas Stacey wrote further: 'Telephones were ringing, ovens roaring and hoovers humming. The church was bursting with human life . . . it spoke of the majesty and power and love of God. . . .'

To some, perhaps, but others might echo Jeremiah:
'They have forsaken me, the fountain of living water,
And hewed out cisterns for themselves,
Broken cisterns that can hold no water.' (2:13)

In devising busy conversions we must keep an eye on the broken cistern aspect. There is no more persistent intrusion upon prayer than a typewriter or a telephone. This alone would be a powerful reason for advocating, wherever practicable, crypt conversions. Churches with partial crypts, disused boiler houses, and so on, could provide catacombs of quiet. Examples of these can be found in London at St Olave's, Hart Street, All Hallows by the Tower, and the chapel converted from a coal hole at 84 Margaret Street. Where the church above has been turned over to noisy use, a prayerful small crypt can redress the balance.

Where the crypt itself is large, it is clearly the more suitable area for conversion. The inspiration for this form of alteration came to Dick Sheppard while he was ministering to the dying in Flanders in the early weeks of the First World War. He gave the eleven people who came to his induction as Vicar of St Martin in the Fields in November 1914 an account of his vision: 'I stood on the west steps and saw what this church would be . . . I saw it full of people, dropping in at all hours of the day and night . . . and I said to them as they passed: "Where are you going?" and they said only one thing: "This is our home . . ."' (R. Ellis Roberts *H. R. L. Sheppard* London 1942, pp. 91 & 102). In October 1916 he opened the church all night for soldiers waiting for trains, for the homeless, for anyone in need of shelter. The role of St Martin in the Fields has grown from these roots. 25 per cent of the youth club who now meet together in the extensive mortuary crypts are regular attendants in the church above. But it is not palatial facilities that hold together a range of activities – scouts, clubs, discothèques – it is strong spiritual leadership. Young people look for it; tycoons recognize it. It attracts. Without it, even office letting falls away. The example of St Martin in the Fields

224. Terrington St John, Norfolk. Mediaeval priest's house between nave and tower

has been followed since the Second World War in, for example, the work for down-and-outs in the undercroft of the John Street chapel in Glasgow, for alcoholics in the crypt of Christchurch, Spitalfields (architect, Cecil Brown) and at St Giles, Camberwell (architect, David Bush). The opposite approach has been adopted at St Peter's, Walworth, where Paul Jobson has converted his crypt into a very popular pub. The architect Raymond Hall has designated the crypt for lively activities in his scheme for the interior of St Matthew's, Brixton. The development of the crypt is the key to Robert Potter's thinking for All Soul's, Langham Place, and for St Stephen's, Walbrook, where excavation is dictated by structural necessity.

The full rehabilitation of crypts can only be beneficial to the structures above them. Their low ceilings diminish heating problems. They can take any weight on the floor. They are good sound-containers or excluders. Their development cannot impair the appearance of the church above them.

But in all other adaptations aesthetic and pastoral considerations have to be carefully weighed. The language of beauty is of the essence of religion, and no one ever built a church without hoping, however remotely, to touch the hem of it. This language can be seriously distorted by partitions, however discreet, however practical. Of course no architect worth his salt is prepared to put into our ancient churches divisions which could not be removed by another generation – unless, as at St Mary's, Sunbury (architect, Charles Brown) they are also serving to hold the church together structurally.

External accretions are another matter. Gathering all parochial structures into the churchyard has administrative advantages, but the French provision of *quartiers sauvegardes* within the immediate prospect of ancient monuments has much to commend it. We who, in these matters, have not safeguarded St Paul's Cathedral, can hardly have been expected to bother about Yatton in Somerset. In fact, the Yatton experiment has much to commend it. No apologetic lean-to, no scramble of variegated building materials here. It is carefully and ambitiously designed with reference to the strange tower of the church behind it. It provides palatial choir vestries and provision for refreshment of which the very elegance might overawe a village. On the other hand, about half the glorious transepted church is to all intents disused, as services focus on a nave altar. A hundred yards away a stone church hall could perhaps have been restored at no greater cost than the building of the addition. Admittedly the extension is better than the bungalows immediately beyond, but it is nevertheless a rueful comment that few modern buildings can enhance the prospect of a major Perpendicular church. It was a bold try. The ambulatory solution round the west end of Greyfriars Church, Reading, on the other hand, is perhaps Kenneth White's masterpiece. It is deft and modest. Perhaps the moral is that if you have to build onto a mediaeval church – if you really must – keep your head low.

The internal adaptation of our churches has been a strong and courageous feature of the years since 1950, but it has a longer history. The Colosseum in Rome is exceptionally well-preserved because its small units

225. Camberwell, London; St Giles. South London crypt altered by David Bush

readily adapted to domestic usage, and were so used throughout the Middle Ages. Monastic churches were frequently put to domestic use after the Reformation, as can still be seen at Llanthony, Monmouthshire, at Leiston and Bury St Edmunds, Suffolk and at Mount Grace Yorkshire. It would be particularly interesting to know more of adaptations made within the monasteries when numbers fell in the fifteenth century. During its seventeenth-century decline the nave of Old St Paul's was used as a market, and Sir Christopher Wren made provision for the dispossessed stallholders under an external arcade in his first model for the rebuilding. The Court of the Arches was held in St Mary le Bow from the thirteenth century onwards. We do know that provision for the clergy to sleep, even perhaps to live, in rooms over porches and vestries was made during the later Middle Ages (Ashdon, Essex, Woolpit and Blythborough, Suffolk, Cirencester, Gloucestershire). The survival at Terrington St Clement's, Norfolk of traces of a four-storeyed priest's house contrived between the nave and tower provides a significant precedent.

Every vicarage and rectory knows the shape of an encounter with a person in trouble: a talk, a cry, a wash, a cup of tea, a phone call, a creative pause. This diversity of caring can be most ably served by home and church under one roof. It is possible, with great skill, to contrive such a conjunction within even a Wren church without harming its design. The 'invisible rectories' at St Lawrence Jewry, (architect, Cecil Brown) and St Mary le Bow (architect, Lawrence King) were both achieved as a result of war damage, and both include hidden roof gardens. Other applications of this principle are on the drawing board and much to be encouraged. The deliberate ramble of many Victorian churches would lend itself to such treatment without affront. How simply, for instance, it could be designed within the transept of Christchurch, Down Street, Mayfair. The policy could have special importance, moreover, in a village context. Peter Codling has published a simple blueprint for a church/clergy house conversion within a small village church (*Norfolk Churches and Their Future*, ed. Wilhelmine Harrod, 1972). Another scheme for a basic aisleless church is set out here by Peter Cleverly. The parish retains a church of practical size with a gallery extension; bells continue to be rung in the tower; room uses are flexible, and the study can double as the parish meeting room. The priest lives in a beautiful, ancient and practical house. It is perhaps sad that recent years have seen the arrival of so many horrid little vicarages in place of the gracious but impracticable Georgian or Victorian ones. Where reassessment of the

226. Yatton, Somerset; St Mary. Parish room, vestries, etc., added to Perpendicular church

227. City of London; St Lawrence, Jewry. Vicarage concealed over north aisle. By Cecil Brown. Section

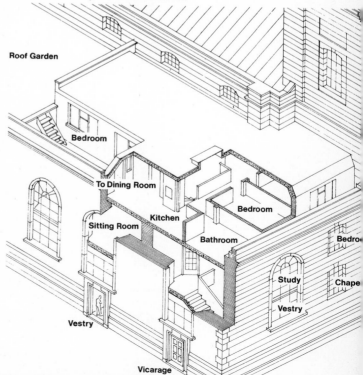

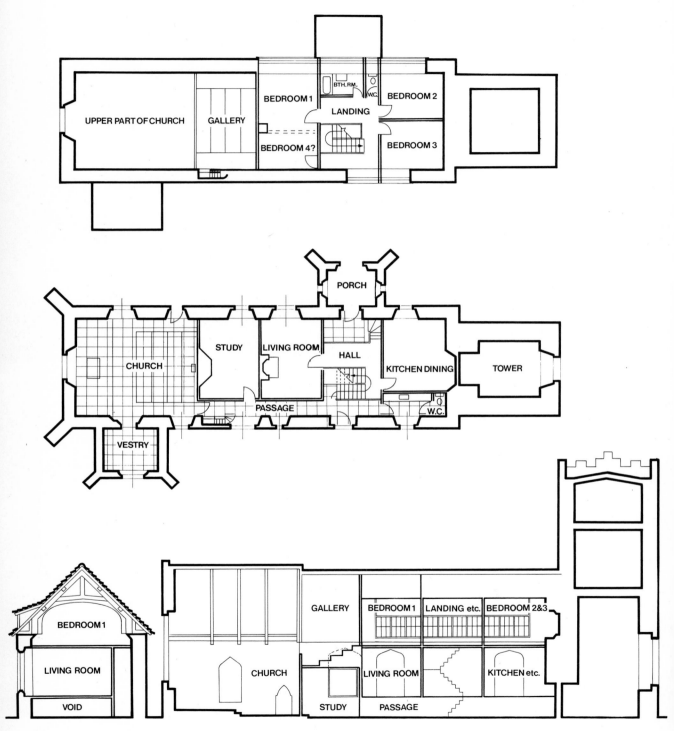

228. Scheme by Peter Cleverly for conversion of a simple country church into a church and vicarage, with parish room/study. The dimensions of the lobby of the church are based on those of St Margaret, Rishangles, Suffolk. Plans and sections

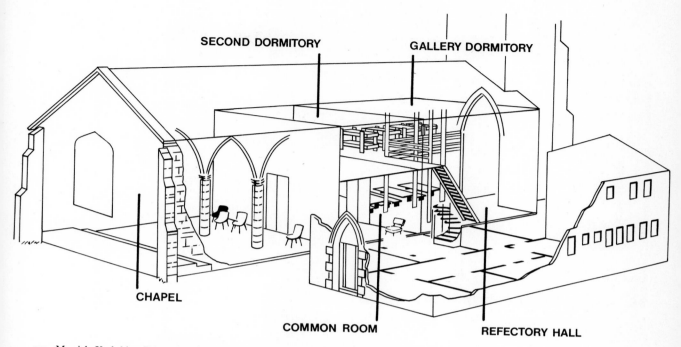

SECOND DORMITORY

GALLERY DORMITORY

CHAPEL

COMMON ROOM

REFECTORY HALL

229. Marrick, Yorkshire; Priory church of St Andrew. Diagram showing conversion into church/youth centre by George Pace

overall situation is still to be made, there is a strong case for the clergy house within the church. As our monastic forebears knew, nothing so revitalizes religion as living in the middle of it. Nor are there many other valid partial alternative uses in a country setting, always excepting that of the duties previously performed by the church hall. Saturation point in art galleries and museums is easily reached. Under the inspiration of Derek Dunn a training centre for stone masonry has been set up at Orton and for sculpture conservation will be established at Little Oakley, Northamptonshire. The Newton in the Willows Field Studies Centre is a total conversion, but the formula has possibilities in the partial alteration context. The study of local history and ecology is growing in our more alert schools: no more natural centre for it than the most ancient local building. The conversion of Marrick Priory, Yorkshire, by George Pace and Partners, is a particularly successful fusion of church and practical living for youth groups.

A village loses its sense of place, its *genius loci*, if it loses its church. Partially converted churches are beginning to play a major role in the establishment of *genius loci* within our amorphous cities. This did not immediately happen with the first wave of post-war alterations within the context of

war damage repairs. The first stage of inner-city conversions was primarily to office use, and with finance somewhat to the forefront. They took place, for the most part, inside churches of broadly classical type – St John's Wood parish church, Holy Trinity, Marylebone Road, St Katharine Cree, St Andrew by the Wardrobe, St Michael's, Paternoster Row, St Mark's, Kennington, St James's, Bermondsey. They adopted the expedient of blocking off aisles and galleries to create offices for organizations related more or less closely to the church. St Mark's, Kennington (architects, the Ford dynasty), where an overhead dome made possible a thorough blocking-off of aisles and galleries, is an example where very full pastoral use is now being made of the facilities provided. A Christian Life College, for example, is one of several activities centred there. The surviving attenuated church interior is fairly gaunt, but Teulon had 'rudely renewed' (according to Pevsner) the interior. Spiritual gains may be said to outweigh architectural losses. Kennington is packed out by full-time Pentecostalism. It could become the first church to regret the curtailing of its seating.

A more flexible partial adaptation by David Nye took place at All Hallows, London Wall in 1962. After a spell as an exhibition centre the nave is now the library of the

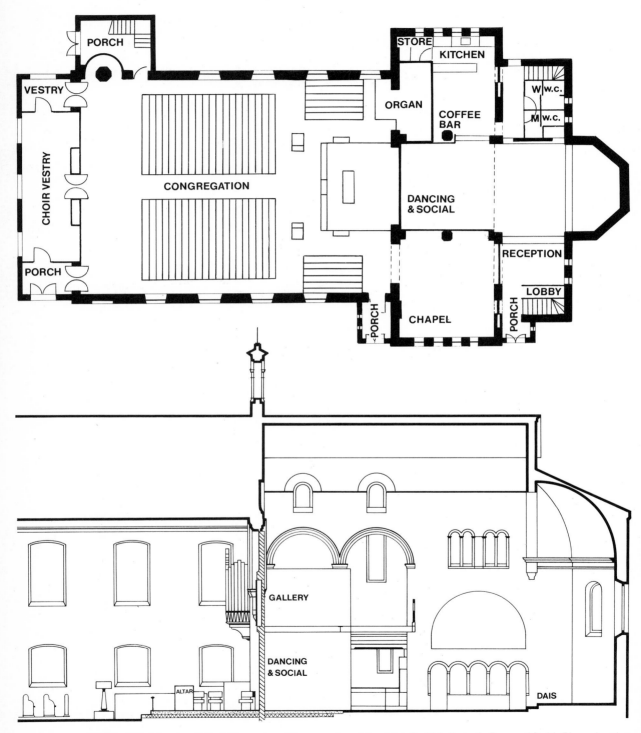

230. Clapham, South London; St Paul. Conversion of Eastern section of church into Parish hall, etc., by Raymond Smith. Plan and section

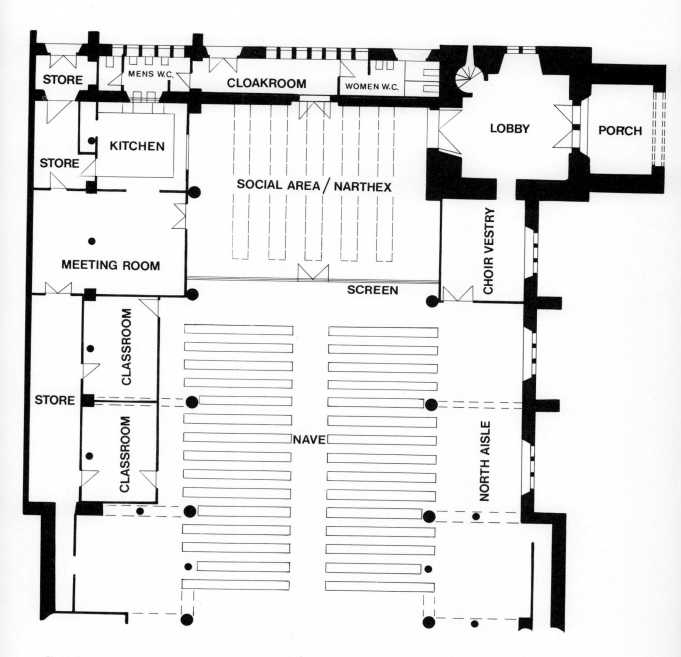

231. Cheltenham, Gloucestershire; St Matthew. Conversion of west end and of the nave by Charles Brown. Plan

Council for Places of Worship, but it is still possible to use almost the whole interior for larger services, small exhibitions and concerts. There are no screens, and the bookcases do not seriously obstruct the view of the most complete church interior designed by George Dance the Younger.

In general it can be strongly argued that churches of the classical type do not take well to lateral partitioning. Their proportions are grievously disarrayed, and the long narrow naves so created are not in keeping with current liturgical modes. On the other hand, the blocking-off of aisles in Victorian Gothic churches is often much happier. The Gothic language takes to contrivance more readily than the classical, and the clerestories remain undisturbed. At Holy Trinity, Upper Tooting the exceptionally wide south aisle was turned into a splendid hall as recently as 1976 (architect, Ford). The cost, thanks to skilled voluntary work, was remarkably low. At St John's, Angell Town, Brixton (Ford) the north aisle makes a very good parish room, to which is appended what ought to be a common feature, a cloakroom for the disabled. At Angell Town as early as 1951 the Fords explored another method of partial conversion: the blocking-off and adaptation of the east end. Kenneth White considered the same solution at Galleywood, Essex and executed it at St Matthew's, Muswell Hill. The two virtues of this line of attack are demonstrated at St Paul's, Clapham (architect Raymond Smith, 1971). Instead of creating a long narrower space, it leaves a short simple one. Where a modest pre-Oxford Movement church has received an elaborate High Victorian chancel – even, as here, by a hand as distinguished as Blomfield's – its visual loss restores a rusticity more in keeping with the recent mood. At St Nicholas, Deptford, the Fords used this method to produce an interior more cogent than it was originally – and created a series of rooms of relatively normal shape behind the altar.

During the last decade emphasis has shifted from the possession of leasable property to the provision of facilities for the congregation to grow to know the clergy and one another, to put down parochial roots. More and more church halls are being closed, and their activities brought under the church roof. The most popular alteration is screening off the west end of the nave, sometimes with the provision of a room above and with extensions into the aisles (St Matthew's, Cheltenham, and St Peter's, Spring Hill, Birmingham, both Charles Brown). The buffer state between church and street is of great strategic value (St Mary's, Balham; Van Lock and R. Smith, 1973). Two tendencies which often march with this alteration – the

acquisition of carpets and jettisoning of irreplaceable wooden pews (to be bought up by pubs for informal seating) – are to be regarded with grave caution. In ecclesiastical terms carpets remain an asset for such a short time, and their maintenance can militate against the very informality they were laid down to foster. Nasty plastic chairs are a non-biodegradeable option, and many who are striplings now may live to regret the comfort and order of a well-cushioned pew. This latter solution is, after all, the common practice in kirks of the Church of Scotland.

There remains one more approach to partial conversion for which Michael Blee's rebuilding after arson of All Saints, Isleworth (1967–70) for Archdeacon Derek Hayward has given us an important prototype. The church was established on the site of the chancel. Offices and vestries within the shell of the nave open onto a central courtyard with a baptistry at the east end. Entry is still through the west tower. Something of the same concept on a different scale, but with flats in place of vestries, is reflected in Biscoe and Stanton's project (1975) for St Barnabas, Addison Road, Kensington. The chancel would remain the church. The nave would be converted into a series of old people's dwellings. Externally, the church would be virtually unaltered. In similar cases the removal of a decayed nave roof could produce a courtyard with dwellings round three sides of it, and the church to the east in the chancel. There are links with the narthex plan of early Christianity, with the almshouse–church relationship at Ewelme. Adaptations as thorough as Biscoe and Stanton's concept for St Barnabas or Thomas Ford's for St Saviour's, Denmark Hill (1976) would not be appropriate in our finest churches. But in many a dim city district the church is the only comely, the only recognizable, silhouette. Better to bring needy lives into it than to pull it down. We have dealt in this way with domestic buildings of the past – the King's Manor, York, Pugin's Albury Park. British architects have a flair for tactful adaptation. Where this gives spiritual life and the cares of living a chance to mingle it is a powerful tool in the hands of the Church, a tool forged of our present poverty, in keeping with our time, and related, like all Christian renewal, to the pattern of the early Church.

The people of Dick Sheppard's visionary procession claimed the church as their home. E. F. Schumacher (*Small is Beautiful* London 1973, pp. 130–31) called those seeking a way based on the beatitudes 'homecomers'. From the husks of bankrupt technology we might return to the Last Friendly House. Partial conversions make sure it is there to receive us.

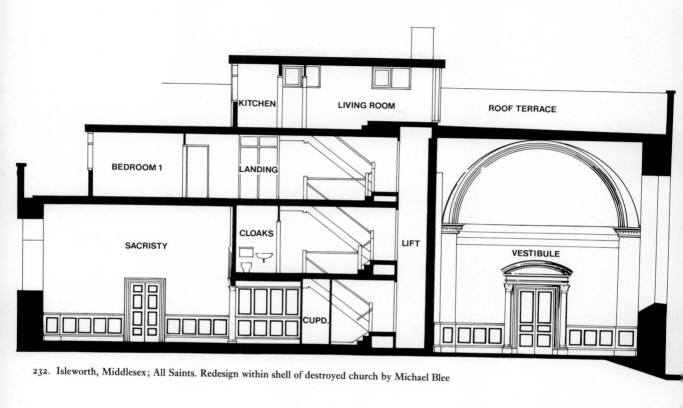

232. Isleworth, Middlesex; All Saints. Redesign within shell of destroyed church by Michael Blee

233. Kensington, London; St Barnabas. Project to convert nave into old people's flats by Biscoe and Stanton

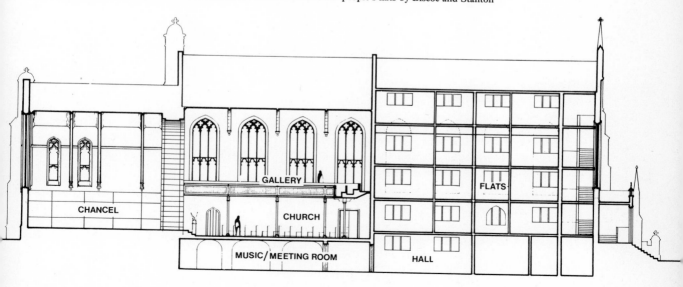

234. Lyscombe, Dorset. A mediaeval chapel, given a temporary roof by a local farmer

235. Pensford, Somerset; St Thomas a Becket. Reprieved after demolition certificate had been granted

WHAT THE INDIVIDUAL CAN DO
by Marcus Binney

There are today some 20 million taxpayers in the United Kingdom: if every one of them gave just one pound a year towards the care and repair of chapels, churches and kirks the problem of maintaining them would be banished overnight – and this is hardly a large sum to ask for the buildings in which some of the most important events in people's lives take place. In Germany such a system exists: if people wish to partake of the rights of the church they must covenant a small proportion of what they pay in income tax to the denomination of their choosing. If they do not they may opt out and pay nothing. In Britain church rates went only to the Established Church, and, owing to understandable pressure from the Nonconformists, were made voluntary as long ago as 1868. The best that can now be hoped for is the beginning of state aid for repairs to historic churches – up to £1m at 1973 prices has been promised. Yet splendid though this is even this will do little more than even out the £1.6m the state is now collecting in Value Added Tax on repairs to churches.

The care of churches will therefore inevitably continue to be largely dependent on voluntary effort and generosity. Obviously the first and most important thing any individual can do is to attend and support his local church, but there are many other ways of contributing to churches in need, and other things to be done besides dipping in one's pocket to save a church from closure or demolition. For while it takes many people to close a church – archdeacons, elders, diocesan committees, presbyteries, circuits – it takes only one determined person – or a small group – to save it. At Fenton in Lincolnshire a little mediaeval church untouched by Victorian restoration lay abandoned and almost derelict until 1971 when the young couple who had just bought the house next door set about cleaning and clearing it of a decade of debris and bird droppings. By involving other villagers they brought back

a sense of community spirit in a village that had almost lost it and since then the church has provided the focus for a steady series of village events. At Kelshall, near Royston, Hertfordshire the parish church was threatened with almost certain closure until the farmer who lived nearby set about raising money for it, and within a short time collected £2500. At Little Bentley in Essex, when the vicar declared his intention of making the church redundant a village committee was formed, and virtually the whole village – sixty to eighty people – turned up to discuss proposals for repairing it. Within a few months they had raised two thirds of the £6,500 needed. At Little Lindford in Buckinghamshire steady decline in the population left the church with only two regular attenders and a repair bill of £1,950. The diocese wanted to make the church redundant but the villagers petitioned the Church Commissioners – at first without success – on the grounds that the building of Milton Keynes would bring more people to the area. An appeal brought money from America and Canada after the church's plight had been featured on television. When essential repairs had been carried out – a local builder helping without payment – the Church Commissioners granted a reprieve.

Again and again the principal obstacle has not been the raising of money but the determination of the ecclesiastical authorities to close or demolish a church, regardless of the wishes of the parshioners. The most famous case is Withiel Florey in Somerset. Following the union of the parish with Brompton Regis an application to demolish was made in 1961 to the consistory court at Taunton. The whole village of some fifty people turned out to give evidence against demolition, except for two elderly people who stayed behind to look after the children. The chancellor decided that the church could stay if a trust was set up to keep it in good repair: this has been done and services are held twice a month. Holnest in Dorset was another church the diocese wanted to pull down: this was saved at the consistory by a doughty lady parishioner who proved herself as skilful a lawyer as Portia. At Aldershot, Hampshire, parishioners wanting to repair their splendid Victorian church found the vicar in complete opposition to such a project, but at the consistory court in 1974 they won their case and have since had a successful appeal.

The Church of England is the only denomination to have its own procedure accepted by Parliament for dealing with redundancy and demolition. Other denominations have, if the chapel, church or kirk is a 'listed' building, to seek permission to demolish it, just as if it were a secular building. If a church is of any merit yet still not listed it is worth asking the Department of the Environment to consider spot-listing it: many nineteenth-century churches have been listed in this way at the instigation of the Victorian Society. An individual, however, can equally set the same process in motion: Mr Charles Colley-Bailey, a historian in Aston, saved what he believes is Yorkshire's oldest Methodist church, at Aughton, near Rotherhay, by this means in 1975. Soon after he saved a much older chapel at St Giles on the Rother from destruction by open

cast mining. Following his representations to the Department of the Environment the National Coal Board was ordered to exclude the land around the chapel from the work and make provision for archaeological excavation.

A particular problem with church buildings is the cloak of secrecy which often surrounds all deliberations about their future even though they are very much public buildings. Here local newspapers provide a vital forum for bringing matters into the open. Few people in Brentwood, Essex, knew that the unusual Warley barracks chapel on the edge of the town, designed in the style of an early Christian basilica by Sir Matthew Digby Wyatt, was under threat until the news was leaked to the local newspaper in September 1976. Hurriedly the vicar of Brentwood and the regimental secretary admitted they had been having discussions on the subject for some eighteen months. The news brought strong reactions from local residents. 'I will do anything in my power to stop this priceless building going,' said one former councillor. An appeal by a local resident to save the splendid United Reform church at Lightcliffe near Halifax from demolition – a building in very sound condition – brought reports first in the local press, then the county newspaper and the next

236. Warley, Essex; Barracks Chapel. A church reprieved by a dramatic local campaign

day on Yorkshire television. A storm in the press gained a last-minute reprieve for Decimus Burton's Holy Trinity church, Tunbridge Wells, listed Grade A, which the Church Commissioners proposed to demolish after a waiting period of only one year. Since then an appeal has been successfully launched for funds to turn it into an arts centre. At Little Salmonby in Lincolnshire the Church Commissioners had actually invited tenders to demolish when a group of local people won a reprieve by offering to form a group of Friends to take over the church.

The formation of groups of Friends has been the saving of a number of churches without a future. The first to be saved in this way was the mediaeval church of Wolfhamcote, near Rugby, Warwickshire, which the Church Commissioners were considering stripping of its fittings so that it could be turned into a house. Following repair the church was vested in the Redundant Churches Fund. The parent body of all such groups is the aptly named Friends of Friendless Churches. The Friends' policy is to help any deserving church regardless of its pastoral future, whatever its denomination. Each year the Friends run appeals for two churches, and since their foundation in 1957 have been instrumental in saving over a 100 churches including a number in Wales.

Good work has also been done by individual county historic churches trusts. These exist in Buckinghamshire, Cheshire, Cornwall, Devon, Dorset, Essex, Herefordshire, Kent, Leicestershire, Lincolnshire, Norfolk, Northamptonshire, Oxfordshire, Rutland, Staffordshire, Suffolk, Sussex and Wiltshire – but why, one asks, not in Berkshire, Cambridgeshire, Gloucestershire, Hampshire, Somerset and Yorkshire – all prosperous counties with many worthwhile churches. Working on a county rather than a parish basis, such trusts can approach charitable foundations and large commercial enterprises which might find it invidious to single out a church for aid. Individual city trusts exist in Norwich and York – two cities with large numbers of mediaeval churches – but these could serve as a model for great northern cities like Leeds, Liverpool and Manchester which have numerous outstanding Victorian churches. Usually such cities have active local civic societies but these tend either to have no money to invest in repairing historic buildings or to invest their funds in a portfolio.

Scotland and Wales, by comparison with England, are at a considerable disadvantage in voluntary bodies concerned with churches. The Scottish Civic Trust, the Scottish Georgian Group and the Council for the Protection of Rural Wales do admirable lobbying on threatened buildings but in neither country is there any equivalent of

237. Lightcliffe, Yorkshire; United Reformed Church. The subject of a major local battle

238. Salmonby, Lincolnshire; St Margaret. Saved by local people after tenders for demolition had been invited

either the Historic Churches Preservation Trust or the Redundant Churches Fund. Both Glasgow and Edinburgh stand second only to London in the number, diversity and importance of their churches, and would be enormously helped by the foundation of city churches trusts.

Local societies and trusts also carry out invaluable rescue work in cleaning and clearing out abandoned churches. The Society for the Protection of Ancient Buildings has organized summer working parties to a number of churches: recently the Norfolk Churches Trust has been very active in this way. At East Horndon in Essex a group of Friends protected a remarkable early Tudor church from vandalism while the church was vulnerable during repair by almost hourly patrols.

The individual can also do a great deal in the way of recording. The National Association of Decorative and Fine Art Societies has a group of Church Recorders which has made admirable inventories of the contents of a number of churches, with guidance from the Victoria and Albert Museum. On several occasions these have helped the police in recovering stolen church property. In Lincolnshire a special project is now underway to record the contents of all parish churches in the county. Volunteers can also provide invaluable help in recording the inscriptions on tombstones before they become illegible through weathering, or indeed are moved or broken. An instructive booklet on the subject has been published by the Council of British Archaeology: another is being prepared by the Society of Genealogists.

Equally important are comprehensive photographic records of churches, showing them both in detail and in their setting, and covering all their major fittings. The National Monuments Record for England now takes good photographs of all redundant Church of England churches, as well as many threatened churches of other denominations. The otherwise admirable National Monuments Record of Scotland, however, is still weak on churches. Competent individual photographers willing to work on a voluntary basis can play a significant role in building up these major national archives. In many cases they will be given a free set of prints in return for the loan

239. Wolfhamcote, Warwickshire. One of the first to be rescued by a group of local Friends

of good negatives. There is also clearly a case for libraries with local history collections to build up photographic records of churches of all denominations: here Liverpool City Library has set an admirable example by commissioning photographs of all the churches in the city.

The individual is helping simply by looking at churches: a steady stream of visitors makes it more likely a church will be open, a full visitors' book will reassure the incumbent and the congregation that the effort of keeping up an old church is worthwhile. Where a church has many visitors the collection box can make a substantial contribution to upkeep. This is particularly notable in churches near country houses and ancient monuments open to the public; Lanhydrock in Cornwall and Great Witley in Worcestershire are two that have benefited in this way. Local events can also bring unexpected numbers of visitors to churches.

The individual can also contribute much by organizing or patronizing special events at churches – be they flower festivals, organ recitals, concerts of chamber music, choral performances, exhibitions, poetry readings, dramatic presentations, ballet or dance, coffee mornings, or evening lectures. These more than anything bring a church alive and involve the whole community. Extended use such as this, unlike adapted use or new use, discussed in previous chapters, does not involve any structural alterations, and allows the whole church to continue in use for worship. Every year at Aldeburgh, Suffolk, two or three churches are used for concerts; at King's Lynn, Norfolk the second great parish church comes to life during the festival. At Edington in Wiltshire there is a festival of liturgical music lasting a week each year. At Highham Ferrers in Northamptonshire the Regional Arts Council supports the annual festival. Some church restorations have been financed almost wholly through church festivals; an example is the church at Ayot St Lawrence, Buckinghamshire, built to look like a temple on the park of the adjoining country house. Here the last two years have brought an almost disused church back to life.

In sum, whatever the problems of churches, there is no lack of ways the imaginative, enterprising and energetic individual can help overcome their plight.

240. Talyllyn Chapel, Anglesey. A Welsh chapel saved with the help of the Friends of Friendless Churches

241. Mundon, Essex. Before repair by the Friends of Friendless Churches

NOTES ON CONTRIBUTORS

DR ROY STRONG is Director of the Victoria and Albert Museum

COLIN McWILLIAM is Chairman of the Scottish Georgian Society and author of *Scottish Townscapes*

ELISABETH BEAZLEY is an architect and author of several books on aspects of Welsh architecture and landscape

JOHN PHYSICK is Keeper of the Museum Services Department at the Victoria and Albert Museum

CLAUDE BLAIR is Keeper of the Department of Metalwork at the Victoria and Albert Museum

SHIRLEY BURY is Deputy Keeper of the Department of Metalwork at the Victoria and Albert Museum

SIMON JERVIS is Deputy Keeper of the Department of Furniture and Woodwork at the Victoria and Albert Museum

MARTIN HARRISON is Curator of Ely Stained Glass Museum

MICHAEL ARCHER is Deputy Keeper of the Department of Ceramics at the Victoria and Albert Museum

MICHAEL GILLINGHAM is an authority on organ cases, and a member of the Organs Advisory Committee of the Council for Places of Worship

PAMELA BURGESS is a writer and consultant on churchyards

THOMAS COCKE is an architectural historian, currently working for Department of the Environment

RICHARD MORRIS is an archaeologist and Secretary of the Council for British Archaeology's Churches Committee

THE VERY REVEREND TONY BRIDGE is Dean of Guildford and a member of the Victoria and Albert Museum's Advisory Council

THE VERY REVEREND R. S. WINGFIELD-DIGBY is Dean of Peterborough and Chairman of Council for Places of Worship

JAMES LEES-MILNE is architectural historian and author of many books

PETER CLEVERLY is an architect in private practice with responsibility for a large number of churches in Suffolk and several major country houses

CANON COLIN SCOTT is Vice Chairman of Southwark Diocesan Pastoral Committee, and a member of Council for Places of Worship

JOHN SCHOFIELD repairs old buildings and is a member of the committee of the Society for the Protection of Ancient Buildings

NICHOLAS COOPER is Deputy Keeper of the National Monuments Record

PATRICK BROWN is an architect and Lecturer to the Department of Architecture, University of Bristol

PAMELA TUDOR-CRAIG is an art historian, member of the Cathedrals Advisory Committee and the London Diocesan Advisory Committee for the Care of Churches

The editors are much indebted to Miss Anne Hills, Secretary to the exhibition, for her help in the preparation of this book.